Philip Hale

Aspects of Forgiveness:

The Basis for Justification and its Modern Denial

PUBLISHED BY MERCINATOR PRESS

MERCINATORPRESS@GMAIL.COM

14205 Ida St.
Omaha NE 68142

Cover illustration: *The Resurrection of Christ*
by Hendrick van den Broeck

Philip Hale.
    Aspects of Forgiveness
        The Basis for Justification and its Modern Denial

  Mercinator Press
    Includes bibliographical references and indexes.
    ISBN: 978-0-9975197-4-7

Contents

Chapter 1

Introduction

The most recent official and public skirmish over justification among conservative Lutherans occurred between two small Lutheran synods in America. Pastor Paul Rydecki was removed from the Wisconsin Evangelical Lutheran Synod (WELS) roster for false doctrine with the charge of having "denied the truth and fallen into error," because he redefined Christ's righteousness which is imputed to sinners.[1] When he joined a very small church body, the Evangelical Lutheran Diocese of North America (ELDoNA), it followed Rydecki's lead on justification, even though many of its pastors were educated in the Lutheran Church Missouri Synod (LCMS) and seemingly held to the teaching of objective justification, the issue of contention. This new public stance of ELDoNA—and a resulting set of theses on the matter[2]—led to broken fellowship ties with another small, no longer extant, body of former Evangelical Lutheran Synod (ELS) congregations. While this fight might seem quite insignificant, it has entangled most morally conservative Lutheran synods of America. Even more, this topic has divided Lutherans substantially for over 150 years. This has become the central debate of the modern era among biblically-minded Lutherans over the most

---

[1] Letter from WELS President Jon Buchholz to Paul A. Rydecki (Oct. 3, 2012; http://ichabodthegloryhasdeparted.blogspot.com/2017/10/rydecki-posts-wels-removal-letter.html).

[2] Evangelical Lutheran Diocese of North America, "Theses on the Article of Justification as Taught in Holy Scripture and the Confessions of Christ's Holy Church with Special Attention to 'Objective Justification'," 2013 Colloquium and Synod (http://www.eldona.org/ELDoNA/Papers_files/Justification_2013.pdf).

important doctrine: justification.

Here are the details of the recent division, which occurred between two minor synods (ELDoNA and The Association of Confessional Lutheran Churches [ACLC[3]]—now defunct):

> The Association of Confessional Lutheran Churches, and the Evangelical Lutheran Diocese of North America recognized fellowship with each other in 2010. At that time neither detected a substantive difference in teaching or practice that would have precluded such a recognition. In the beginning of 2013 the ACLC became aware that the ELDoNA was entertaining an application from Rev. Paul Rydecki for membership into their diocese. We also became aware that the ELDoNA was preparing a set of theses regarding the doctrine of Justification, specifically addressing its objective aspect. Rev. Rydecki had been very vocal about questioning the objective aspect of this chief article of the Christian faith, so we began to request open discussion of that doctrine with the ELDoNA. . . .
>
> As we moved toward recognition of fellowship with the ELDoNA, we did not realize that she was not grounded in what we all had been taught. We naively believed that Objective Justification, as taught in the synods of the old Synodical Conference (LCMS, WELS, and ELS), and confessed in documents such as the "Brief Statement," is so fundamental, so pervasively taught, so clear, that it could not possibly be an issue with anyone coming out of any of those Lutheran bodies.[4]

This skirmish between minor synods might seem technical and abstract, or just an argument over words, but the condemnations of both sides say otherwise.

The declared public fellowship between these two church bodies was broken over this issue of justification:

> We recognize, therefore, that the ELDoNA [by its public adoption of the 2013 "Theses on the Article of Justification"]

---

[3]This now defunct synod, evidently reabsorbed back into the ELS, is not to be confused with the ACELC (Association of Confessing Evangelical Lutheran Congregations), a group of churches within the LCMS aiming for unity by making a doctrinal confession.

[4]Preamble, The Association of Confessional Lutheran Churches, "Critique of the Evangelical Lutheran Diocese of North America's Theses on Justification" (Feb. 9, 2014; http://www.dropbox.com/s/rczja2b8f2k9jgf/ACLC-Official_Critique_of_ELDoNA_Theses_on_Justification.pdf), 2, 13.

has placed the ACLC outside of the lines of her fellowship. The consequences of this are that the ELDoNA and the ACLC are no longer able to exchange pulpits and celebrate Holy Communion together.[5]

This is but a small and recent example of the divisive and explosive nature of this topic. It is one worthy of attention for those who claim to have a pure understanding of this chief article of the Christian religion: the article of justification.

While at first glance, this disagreement might seem like splitting hairs—a topic for theological experts—consider some of the serious charges made:

We [the ACLC] do, however, maintain that a significant roadblock to unity in this doctrine is an inability on the part of the ELDoNA to properly distinguish between Law and Gospel, or at a minimum, a failure to recognize the proper distinction between Law and Gospel in various statements made by others including the Fathers of Lutheran Orthodoxy.[6]

Rydecki made the charge, in reaction to his dismissal from WELS: "I am amazed that you have so directly condemned the Scriptural and Lutheran Gospel of justification by grace through faith and redefined the Gospel of the Lord Jesus Christ to exclude faith from its proclamation. . . . your 'gospel' without faith is not the Gospel."[7] Although some may not see a real issue in this teaching—just a slight nuance in terminology—these quotes show a more substantial disagreement lurking in the background.

But this debate is not even confined to North America. One Lutheran pastor can speak of the "modern (Scandinavian) debate about universal justification."[8] ELDoNA and Rydecki state that the three major

---

[5]ACLC, "Critique of ELDoNA," 34.

[6]ACLC, "Critique of ELDoNA," 4.

[7]Letter from Paul Rydecki to President Jon Buchholz and the AZ-CA District Presidium (Oct. 15, 2012; http://ichabodthegloryhasdeparted.blogspot.com/2012/10/letter-to-wels-district-president-jon.html).

[8]Magnus N. Sørensen, "The Justification of Christ as the Efficient Cause of our Justification—the Narrow Lutheran Middle in the Controversy on Universal Objective Justification," 2017 Convocation of the Orthodox Lutheran Confessional Conference (http://www.academia.edu/34121363/The_Justification_of_Christ_as_the_Efficient_Cause_of_Our_Justification_-The_Narrow_Lutheran_Middle_in_the_Controversy_on_Universal_Objective_Justification),

conservative Lutheran synods in the U.S. today (LCMS, WELS, ELS) have been wrong since their beginning. They not only claim all of these churches have been misled, but suggest that they have even invented this teaching.[9]

Why should one care? Because justification is the central teaching of the Lutheran church, without which there is no hope, forgiveness, or Christianity.

> This article is in a sense the stronghold and the high fortress of all the doctrine and of the entire Christian religion; if it is obscured or adulterated or set aside, the purity of doctrine in other articles of faith cannot possibly be maintained. But if this article is kept pure, all idolatry, superstitions, and whatever corruptions there are in other articles of faith tumble down of their own weight.[10]

Deformities in this doctrine change the nature of faith, forgiveness, and the Gospel itself. God's Word shows us the serious consequences of holding or tolerating another gospel:

> I am astonished that you are so quickly deserting him who called you in the grace of Christ and are turning to a different gospel—not that there is another one, but there are some who trouble you and want to distort the gospel of Christ. But even if we or an angel from heaven should preach to you a gospel contrary to the one we preached to you, let him be accursed. As we have said before, so now I say again: If anyone is preaching to you a gospel contrary to the one you received, let him be accursed (Gal. 1:6–9).

The main issue in justification today is the effect of Christ's work and how the results of His atonement are applied to sinners. Since the Reformation, the main topic of contention has been justification, but the debate has moved backwards from the reception of forgiveness by one's faith to its basis and foundation in Christ. The crux of justification, over the last 150 years and more, is the ground of forgiveness, which defines the Gospel and to whom it may be spoken. These are the main points of contention among Lutherans, not the righteousness of works versus faith in the classic, pharisaic sense used against Rome.

15.

[9]See page 84.

[10]Martin Chemnitz, *Loci Theologici*, quoted in: Robert Preus, "Justification as Taught by Post-Reformation Lutheran Theologians" (March 26, 1982; http://archive. org/details/JustificationAsTaughtByPost-reformationLutheranTheologians), 1.

While this may appear to be a new debate, many still remember the fallout of the 1979 Kokomo affair[11] in WELS and the troubles with the same concern shortly thereafter in the LCMS at its Fort Wayne seminary. In actuality, this disagreement on the foundation and extent of justification is a long-standing controversy that has been simmering for over 150 years. It has not always been at the surface and forefront, but it has been the most divisive doctrinal issue among conservative-leaning Lutherans. The crucial teaching of the application and extent of salvation serves, in fact, as a summary and history of modern Lutheranism. As Walther pinpoints in his masterful 1872 Synodical Conference essay: "A main question in this whole topic is: What is the Gospel?"[12] This is not merely an academic debate: it gets to the heart of Christianity and the bedrock of our hope in Christ. Therefore, it is necessary to get it right.

---

[11]See p. 80.

[12]C.F.W. Walther, *Justification—Objective and Subjective: A Translation of the Doctrinal Essay Read at the First Convention of the Synodical Conference in 1872*, trans. Kurt Marquart (Fort Wayne: Concordia Seminary Press; http://www.angelfire. com/ny4/djw/JustificationObjectiveSubjectiveMarquart.pdf), 30.

Chapter 2

The Dual Nature of Redemption Language

Scripture is God's Word and the standard for all speaking about Christian doctrine. True theology follows the biblical pattern of teaching, even when disparate verses do not conform to our logical expectations. That is the root of this debate, which is not a new concern: What does Scripture say about justification before Christ's righteousness is individually appropriated by faith? In other words: Is Christ's redemptive work the direct cause, source, and origin of our justification, or does faith make the forgiveness of sins a reality, activating the payment Christ made, and thereby satisfying God, only when an individual sinner believes? These are significant questions that are not easily navigated. What Scripture says is clear, but it is easily twisted by sinners whose sinful nature cannot receive the truth without the Spirit.

To introduce the topic of justification, it is helpful to look at the duality of other scriptural words. Who is redeemed? All the world was redeemed by Christ's action: "in [Christ] we have redemption, the forgiveness of sins" (Col. 1:14). Christ was the price with which all mankind's sins were paid. "A death has occurred that redeems them from the transgressions committed under the first covenant" (Heb. 9:15). Blood signifies His death and the sacrifice He made for our sins. "In him we have redemption through his blood, the forgiveness of our trespasses, according to the riches of his grace" (Eph. 1:7). Believers partake of and possess this redemption and forgiveness in faith, but the sins of the whole world were atoned for in His death: "He is the propitiation for our sins, and not for ours only but also for the sins of the whole world" (1 Jn. 2:2).

Is Christ truly the Redeemer and Savior of all, even though not all actually believe the Gospel and achieve paradise? "For to this end we toil and strive, because we have our hope set on the living God, who is the Savior of all people, especially of those who believe" (1 Tim. 4:10). Stated another way: Is Christ dependent on man to be the Savior of all? The difficulty starts in defining how the universal role of Christ as the Redeemer of the world applies to humanity. If Christ, the world's redeemer, has already completed redemption for all, are all redeemed personally? No; that would be universalism, which is unbiblical. Unbelief condemns, and those outside of Christ have no share in His salvation: "Whoever believes and is baptized will be saved, but whoever does not believe will be condemned" (Mk. 16:16). Without the faith the Spirit works in each believer, the sinner is under God's wrath and condemnation.

But Scripture still calls Christ "Redeemer," despite the fact that not all are personally redeemed (Job 19:26; Is. 63:16). Jesus is rightly confessed to be "the Lamb of God, who takes away the sin of the world" (Jn. 1:29). So the world's sins are taken away (forgiven) in Christ, yet, for individual unbelievers, their sins and God's wrath remains on them, condemning them. Christ completed redemption in His death and resurrection for all those under the law. "Christ redeemed us from the curse of the law" and "God sent forth his Son, born of woman, born under the law, to redeem those who were under the law" (Gal. 3:13; 4:4–5). This redemption is complete, from the vantage point of Christ's work. Without faith, however, no one benefits from Christ's universal redemption.

Both strands and emphases—the completeness of salvation from God's side and the necessary beneficial reception from man's side— must be upheld to give the full biblical picture of salvation. A one-sided emphasis cannot capture this full picture. In fact, isolating one facet as the only one leads to heresy. Although many verses do not, some Scripture passages do indicate the "universality of salvation."[1] But

---

[1]Martin H. Franzmann, "Reconciliation and Justification," *Concordia Theological Monthly* XXI:2 (Feb. 1950; http://www.ctsfw.net/media/pdfs/

salvation is not an idea or axiom to make inferences from—it is truly an accomplished reality in Christ's crucified body, which was resurrected for our justification. "[Christ] was delivered up for our trespasses and raised for our justification" (Rom. 4:25). The critical question is not the context of this verse, but doctrinally who was Christ raised for, and what sort of justification applies to man as a result of Christ's coming to life. All of Scripture, not human logic, must paint the correct picture of the scope and wholeness of salvation.

Here is a helpful description of the fluidity of salvation terms in the Bible:

> Some terms that Scripture uses to describe facets of God's plan of salvation are universal terms, and they are always universally applicable. Words like *atonement, propitiation, expiation,* and *payment* are applicable in Christ to the entire world. Lutherans would never use these terms in the exclusive sense to limit their effect only to believers. We always teach universal atonement, universal propitiation, etc. These words form the unshakable foundation for the conviction that sin has been completely removed for all people in Christ.
>
> Other theological terms are only exclusive and can only be used as they apply to individual sinners. We can never use them in a universal way, as if they applied to the whole world. When they are used collectively, they refer to a specific subset of the world, namely to those who have faith in Jesus as their Savior. *Regeneration* can only describe the new birth that believers have experienced as they have been brought to life by the Holy Spirit. *Imputation* typically is the process of crediting something to someone. It is unclear to say that God has imputed Christ's righteousness to everyone, when behind the idea of an imputation is the idea of a positive balance transfer. Fleshing out the metaphor, the world doesn't have an account with God; an individual has an account. *Adoption* is the effect of God's claim upon a believer as a new member of his family, the household of believers. God has not adopted the world. *Sanctification* we recognize as the work of the Holy Spirit and a fruit of faith. . . . A *saint* is someone who has been set apart as holy and devoted to the Lord God. Since the Holy Spirit has not worked faith in the heart of everyone in the world, nor has everyone been set apart as holy, we cannot use the word sanctification in a universal sense.
>
> Some words are used in both a universal and an individual

FranzmannReconciliationJustification.pdf), 88.

sense. They can refer both to the world in its totality and to particular sinners individually. *Reconciliation* is one such word that is used both ways.[2]

Redemption, salvation, and grace are for all. They are all universal, as they exist in Christ. Jn. 3:16 describes the love that motivated the Father to send the Son to atone for the sins of all: "For God so loved the world, that he gave his only Son, that whoever believes in him should not perish but have eternal life." As a result of Christ's work, grace—God's favor and acceptance—is available for all. Most Christians rightly hold the work of Christ—as described by words like atonement, propitiation, expiation, and payment—as universal.

But the reception of Christ's work by the individual is only had by faith, the possession of the Holy Spirit. Sanctification, renewal, regeneration, adoption, and imputation describe the appropriation and reception of the fruit of Christ's work. They all mark personal possession.

The results of Christ's work can be differentiated from the work itself. The consequences of Christ's atonement occupy that middle ground between the universal and the individual dimensions of salvation. In other words, they are both universal and personal.

There are two sides to every relationship: no one can have a relationship completely independent of another. If a debt must be paid, then there must be one to whom the debt is owed. Who accepted the payment of Christ's work, the price of our redemption? The Father, who asserted the finality and completion of our redemption when He raised Jesus to life. Now God's anger over sin and divine justice is appeased through Christ. This message of the finality of redemption in Christ is the Gospel.

Since there are two sides to every relationship, there are also two ways of describing the relation between God and man. Both forgiveness and reconciliation can be viewed from God's side and from man's side. From God's side, justification and salvation are universal—they apply to the entire world. Christ's payment and work is complete and final. From the vantage point of Christ's work, there is nothing lacking. In this sense, "no sharp line is to be drawn between Reconciliation and

---

[2]Jon D. Buchholz, "Jesus Canceled Your Debt!" (2012; http://essays.wls.wels. net/bitstream/handle/123456789/950/BuchholzJustification.pdf), 25.

Justification, . . . both terms refer to the same act of God in Christ."[3] This meal is complete and stands ready for faith to eat in the Gospel. "And the bread that I will give for the life of the world is my flesh" (Jn. 6:51).

The victory of Christ is spoken of in both universal and personal terms. "Now is the judgment of this world; now will the ruler of this world be cast out" (Jn. 12:31). Satan is judged, and sin and death are defeated. The victory becomes our victory in faith, as Christ's salvation becomes ours; "For everyone who has been born of God overcomes the world. And this is the victory that has overcome the world—our faith" (1 Jn. 5:4). Christ's victory is entire and perfect in itself, and is for all people, yet only individuals born of faith possess it for themselves.

The tie between Christ's work and man's reception in faith is the righteousness that results from the accomplished work of Jesus. The Word of God is how that universal promise of redemption comes to us. In this middle ground between the universal and individual aspects of salvation we find the power of the Word, which delivers salvation to us. Though not all hear and believe, Jesus did not fail in His aim: "for I did not come to judge the world but to save the world" (Jn. 12:47). Thus, the world is saved.

Yet, Scripture states that *faith* saves. "And he said to the woman, 'Your faith has saved you; go in peace' " (Lk. 7:50). But that is not the only way Scripture speaks. In fact, prior to saying faith has saved the sinful woman, Jesus declared to her: "Your sins are forgiven" (7:48). Faith is not something apart from Christ; it is this trust in His Word which incorporates us into Him.

It is clear that there is no absolute phrase describing the full picture of salvation. One aspect of the two-sided relationship can be emphasized more or less than the other, but to reproduce the whole of Christ's teaching requires a very careful use of Scripture, lest reason construct its own framework against the revealed Word. Take another use of "save" in Scripture—one that is not popular today: "but the woman was deceived and became a transgressor. Yet she will be saved through childbearing— if they continue in faith and love and holiness, with self-control" (1 Tim. 2:14–15). Childbearing saves, God says explicitly, but that does not

---

[3]Martin Franzmann, "Reconciliation and Justification," 90.

10

automatically damn those females who do not bear children. "Save" can be used in an earthly sense without violating salvation by faith: I saved my keys from the trashcan. So women are saved from Eve's weakness and Satan's deception in this earthly submission to God's procreative work, done in faith, in contrast to exercising Eve-like authority and headship over men. The travails of childbearing and motherhood save women who submit to God's will, in an earthly sense, from rebelliously sinning like Eve and from the weakness of the flesh which always goes against God's created order. Even the possibility of bearing children is a holy and blessed restriction for the Christian woman—not an evil. It is so good, right, and helpful that God says that it "saves." This submission which God witnesses to by biology itself leads to fulfilling the physical role Christ created for women—it does not in the least conflict with salvation by faith in Christ's blessed work. This earthly, and in some ways cursed, role that saves from certain sins and feminine weaknesses can only be accepted, embraced, and loved as a divine duty in the Spirit—who is had by receiving Christ's prior salvation from all guilt and sin. This one example shows that each verse and doctrinal strand in Scripture has the potential for abuse. We must look to the whole of Scripture and put all its aspects together, not ruling out any word of God.

From man's side, faith is necessary for receiving salvation. But faith is not the content of the Gospel, merely how that salvation in Christ is received. Faith is not a substance that man trades with God to get Him off his back. That is why the universal aspect of salvation is critical to preserving the purity of the Gospel. The two ways of speaking "must be as two sides of a single truth: *All men* are justified in Jesus Christ and only *the faithful* are justified in Jesus Christ."[4] Justification is, traditionally and biblically, usually spoken of in terms of individuals. The objective aspect of justification, which is simply forgiveness and its judicial basis, has been denied in this modern era of Christianity, even among Lutherans. The Greek root of "justify" "is neither exclusively objective in the cross nor exclusively subjective in experience. It rather has the objectivity of relationship, enacted at the cross and apprehended

---

[4]Hans Kueng, quoted in: Kurt E. Marquart, "Objective Justification," *Marquart's Works*, 10 vols., ed. Herman J. Otten (New Haven, MO: Lutheran News, 2014–15), 74.

in faith."[5]

The dual nature of redemption creates a problem for man's logic: "How can we possibly say that Christ is the Lamb of God which took away the sins of the world without saying that the sins of the world are forgiven" in some sense.[6] If sins are taken away, they are no longer on the world. This gets to the essence of Christianity: "According to the teaching of the Christian religion man is already redeemed, is already freed from sin and all ill, and God is already reconciled to him."[7] If he is not freed, he must do something to achieve peace with God. Without forgiveness, the relationship is broken from God's side. If God is not reconciled, man must reconcile Him by his efforts.

The closeness of reconciliation—which is widely acknowledged as having two dimensions—to justification is key to understanding it properly. " 'Reconciliation is actualized as justification; justification involves reconciliation.' We go one step farther and say that with the reconciliation the actual absolution of the world's sins has taken place."[8] In one manner of speaking, justification is complete for all mankind (in Christ), yet in its actual reception (by man) it is not had by any apart from faith.

The modern controversy over justification and its objective aspect centers on the word "justification," but involves the two-sided nature of reconciliation—the precise relationship between man and God and how it was affected by Christ's death and resurrection. The denial of any objective side to justification by ELDoNA shows this:

> The reconciliation/justification of the world is already accomplished in Christ in this sense: that what God needs in order to consider each sinner righteous—the exchange of righteousness for sin in Christ—is accomplished; yet, unless the sinner is reconciled to God/justified by God through

---

[5]"δικαιόω," *Theological Dictionary of the New Testament,* ed. Gerhard Kittel, ed. and trans. Geoffrey W. Bromiley (Grand Rapids: Eerdmans, 1964), 2:216.

[6]Siegbert W. Becker, "Objective Justification," Chicago Pastoral Conference, WELS, Elgin, Illinois (Nov. 9, 1982; http://essays.wls.wels.net/bitstream/handle/123456789/331/BeckerJustification.pdf), 11.

[7]Franz Pieper, "C.F.W. Walther as Theologian: Justification, Universal," in *Lehre und Wehre* (Feb. 1890), trans. Wallace McLaughlin (http://backtoluther.blogspot.com/2013/02/walther-as-theologian-justification-by_28.html), 2.

[8]Paul Althaus, quoted in: Martin Franzmann, "Reconciliation and Justification," 90.

> trust in the righteousness of Christ (cf. 2 Cor. 5), he is not indeed reconciled. Since some are not reconciled/justified, it cannot be said that all are reconciled/justified.[9]

"What God needs," the merit or price Christ paid, to actually reconcile is complete, but that is not reconciliation in itself. This is equivalent, logically, to saying that because not all are saved, Jesus is not really the Savior of the world. God's reconciliation to man is left out—as if it is incomplete until faith comes into view. It is not a part of the theological picture for those who have no room in their thinking for a general reconciliation of mankind by Christ: "Jesus is merely seen as someone making an actual payment and not as the one who has taken over the debt itself as our representative and therefore is also the one who receives justification on our behalf."[10] This error shows itself as a matter of prime importance, since it deals with the substitutionary manner of Christ's death and, therefore, His resurrection.

The issue is not the words themselves, but the singular doctrine of Christ. Words can be defined in different ways to speak the fullness of the truth of Scripture. "The terms 'universal' and 'objective' reconciliation have been used by some theologians as essentially synonymous with objective justification. Most notable among them is Franz Pieper [of the Missouri Synod]. . . . "[11] Though the word justification has historically been used to talk of the individual believer's participation in Christ's redemption, it has increasingly been used to highlight the universal dimension of salvation that has been most neglected by Protestants.

This new, churchly use of "justification" disturbs some, but consider that the word "atonement" and its corollaries were historically used

---

[9]ELDoNA, "Theses on the Article of Justification," 28.

[10]Magnus Sørensen, "The Justification of Christ," 25.

[11]Rick Nicholas Curia, *The Significant History of the Doctrine of Objective or Universal Justification among the Churches of the Former Evangelical Lutheran Synodical Conference of North America* (1983; http://archive.org/details/TheSignificantHistoryOfTheDoctrineOfObjectiveOrUniversalJustification), 4. Others in the Missouri tradition do make a distinction: "Through this reconciliation God has only made it possible for Himself to impart to sinful man further demonstrations of His grace. He has so far suppressed His wrath that He further concerns Himself with the sinners of the world. Reconciliation has opened the way for the possibility of the forgiveness of sins, of justification." George Stoeckhardt, "General Justification," trans. Otto F. Stahlke, *CTQ* 42:2 (April 1978; http://ctsfwmedia.s3.amazonaws.com/CTQ/CTQ%2042-2.pdf), 139.

in such a way to include the objective aspect of redemption. Christ's atonement was often used in the sense of not only what Christ did to earn forgiveness, but also its immediate effects, the forgiveness and life the reconciled Father bestows. What often was conflated throughout history, Christ's atoning work and its effects and consequences, now must be distinguished in response to new heresies. This is evidenced by a 19th century non-Lutheran, who says the same in his book on the atonement: "The Preaching of Forgiveness [is] based on the Atonement, and [is] ever connected with the Atonement."[12] This truth is shown from Jesus' institution of the Supper: "this is my blood of the covenant, which is poured out for many for the forgiveness of sins" (Matt. 26:28). The same Scottish author wrote a list describing the scope of Christ's atonement:

> The atonement of the Lord, or the finished work of redemption, glorifies God on the earth, or gives the supreme God the glory due to His name, as the tribute or revenue from His creatures. (5) The Lord Jesus, by means of His humiliation unto death, opened heaven, and brought men and angels, heretofore separated and estranged, into a new relation. (6) The atonement is called the judgment of the world, and the victory by which the Lord overcame the world. (7) The atoning death of Jesus is declared to have judged and cast out the prince of this world. (8) It overcomes the power of death and the fear of death.[13]

The effects of Christ's atonement, which apply and avail for all mankind, cannot ever be fully disconnected from Christ's work, but they are now commonly distinguished, since they cannot be assumed in the face of their outright denial.

What was conflated throughout history, the dual aspect of the price and the benefits of the atonement, must now be separated, lest they be lost completely. Older Lutheran theologians most definitely acknowledged not just the possibility of man using the atonement for his benefit, but the universal effect of the atonement, which applies to all men. "To be sure, it is not to be denied that Scripture in several places speaks of justification as of a universal benefit of grace of God upon all men"

---

[12]George Smeaton, *The Doctrine of the Atonement as Taught by Christ Himself* (Edinburgh: T & T Clark; 2nd ed., 1871; reprint, Grand Rapids: Zondervan, 1953; http://archive.org/details/docofatone00smeauoft), xv.

[13]George Smeaton, *The Doctrine of the Atonement as Taught by Christ Himself*, 284.

(Rom. 5:18, 2 Cor. 5:19).[14] An older dogmatician, Abraham Calov, also makes this same distinction in his comment on 2 Cor. 5:19: "Therefore the kind of reconciliation into which Christians are encouraged to enter is different from the reconciliation of the world, which Christ already accomplished. The former kind of reconciliation is necessarily based on that kind of reconciliation, which already happened and which God has presented to us."[15] This is not just the general grace or love of God—that He wants man to be saved—but the fact that the actual judicial relation of God to the world has been altered in Christ. This is what is called the justification of the world, or objective justification. This speaks not to the *payment*, but the *immediate effect* of Christ's atoning work: "It is God's response [that] His anger has been stilled and He is at peace with the world, and therefore He has declared the entire world in Christ to be righteous."[16] This objective aspect of justification corresponds to the restoration of God's relationship to man.

> The reconciliation of the whole world is the justification of the whole world. . . . As soon as the reconciliation of the world had been effected through Christ, at that moment the forgiveness of sins and the justification of the whole world was an accomplished fact; at that moment justification unto life came upon all men. . . . [17]

This is the plain teaching of 2 Cor. 5:19: "in Christ God was reconciling the world to himself, not counting their trespasses against them. . . . " This part of the verse explains one side of the relationship—from God to man, but not man to God. Trespasses are not counted, or imputed,

---

[14]Philipp David Burk (1714–1770), quoted in: Walther, *Justification—Objective and Subjective*, 21. A denier of objective justification wants to trace this supposed error to him, failing to see it in Luther and throughout history, claiming that Burk "may be the inventor of objective justification." Gregory L. Jackson, *Luther versus the Pietists: Justification by Faith* (Martin Chemnitz Press; Revised 2012), 18.

[15]Abraham Calov, "Thoughts on Objective Justification: Selections from Abraham Calov's *Biblia Illustrata*: 2 Corinthians 5:18–19; Romans 3:23–24, 4:25, and 5:18–19," trans. Souksamay K. Phetsanghane, Southwestern Conference of the Western Wisconsin District, WELS, Winter Conference, Baraboo, WI (Feb. 25, 2014; http://essays.wls.wels.net/handle/123456789/989), 11.

[16]Robert D. Preus, "Objective Justification," *Concordia Theological Seminary Newsletter* (Spring 1981; http://ichabodthegloryhasdeparted.blogspot.com/2015/12/synergism-its-logical-association-with.html; also: http://www.angelfire.com/ny4/djw/PreusJustification.html).

[17]Carl Manthey Zorn (1846–1928), quoted in: Rick Curia, *History of Objective or Universal Justification*, 59.

in Christ. This is all God's action through the Savior of the world. The second part of the same verse speaks of the subjective aspect of justification: " . . . and entrusting to us the message of reconciliation." This forgiveness in Christ is taken possession of when the message is heard and faith is created.

Rom. 5 speaks of reconciliation as a past, completed act, and also as a present reality for individuals in time: "For if while we were enemies we were reconciled to God by the death of his Son, much more, now that we are reconciled, shall we be saved by his life. More than that, we also rejoice in God through our Lord Jesus Christ, through whom we have now received reconciliation" (10–11). This chapter of Romans continues later:

> And the free gift is not like the result of that one man's sin. For the judgment following one trespass brought condemnation, but the free gift following many trespasses brought justification. For if, because of one man's trespass, death reigned through that one man, much more will those who receive the abundance of grace and the free gift of righteousness reign in life through the one man Jesus Christ.
>
> Therefore, as one trespass led to condemnation for all men, so one act of righteousness leads to justification and life for all men. For as by the one man's disobedience the many were made sinners, so by the one man's obedience the many will be made righteous (16–19).

As all become sinners in Adam, all are righteous in Christ. The ESV adds verbs of differing tenses to v18, even though there are no stated verbs at all: "Therefore, as one trespass *led* to condemnation for all men, so one act of righteousness *leads* to justification and life for all men." The original has no verbs, as they are implied: "Therefore as by the guilt of one into all men into condemnation, so by the [righteousness] of one into all men into justifying of life."[18] Another translation takes the parallel between Adam and Christ implied by the text quite seriously: "In other words, just as it was through one offence that all people came under condemnation, so also it is through one righteous act that all people come to be considered righteous."[19] The consequence of Christ's

---

[18] *Wycliffe's Bible: A Modern-Spelling Version of the 14th Century Middle English Translation* (2012; http://www.biblegateway.com).

[19] David H. Stern, *Complete Jewish Bible* (Messianic Jewish Publishers, 1998; http://www.biblegateway.com).

work, according to Rom. 5, extends to all people, as does the result of Adam's sin. These two different verdicts or judgments are universal in application, without opposing each other.

Condemnation in Adam and righteousness in Christ are not conflicting, because they speak from two different sides: God's relation to man and man's relation to God. "As in Adam all men have fallen and come under the wrath of God and eternal damnation as punishment for sins, so also all men are truly redeemed from sin, death, devil and hell, in Christ as the second Adam, and God is truly reconciled with them all."[20] All men are redeemed, but this is not true from man's side—all men are truly cursed, born into wrath. "We are by nature children of wrath" (Eph. 2:3). To receive a share in and personally possess forgiveness requires a second birth, given in Baptism. From God's side, excluding individuals, righteousness is just as universal as the condemnation of sin is in Adam. God sets Christ and Adam in parallel as far as the extent of their respective work: "Paul here is comparing Adam and Christ in equal fashion: it is impossible that Christ could make less people righteous than Adam made sinners."[21] Today, this is commonly termed "objective justification." But it is just one piece of the scriptural puzzle—one that can never be fully separated from the reception of justification in faith: "As soon as a man is a man he is indeed in possession of the curse, but he is not similarly also at once in possession of the merit of Christ. The treasure is indeed there for all men, the debt of all is paid, so that in the blood of Christ all men's righteousness, life, and salvation are brought back."[22] The phrase "in Christ" is crucial: all the world is righteous in Christ, but we are not in Christ simply by being human, because we are born into Adam.

The origin of each verdict does not speak to how we are to be in Christ: "Therefore, since we have been justified by faith, we have peace with God through our Lord Jesus Christ. Through him we have also obtained access by faith into this grace in which we stand, and we rejoice in hope of the glory of God" (Rom. 5:1–2). This standing we have in Christ, and our access to the Father through Him, speaks of our personal reconciliation to the already reconciled God—the possession

---

[20]Walther, *Justification—Objective and Subjective*, 8.

[21]Sebastian Schmidt (1617–1696), quoted in: Robert Preus, "Justification as Taught by Post-Reformation Lutheran Theologians," 9.

[22]Walther, *Justification—Objective and Subjective*, 9.

of salvation. This is commonly termed "subjective justification," which is the personal appropriation of what is valid for all humanity in Christ. As we can speak of mankind's redemption, salvation, and reconciliation, so also God speaks of humanity's forgiveness, or justification, in Christ.

There are different aspects, dimensions, and ways of analyzing justification. Here is a succinct summary: "Objective Justification is the Father's declaration that He has accepted what Christ has done in the Atonement. Subjective Justification believes what Objective Justification declares, for justifying faith must have an object, or it is in vain, and does not justify."[23] Justification is a multifaceted word in Scripture. It is used both with faith and without any connection to faith. All mankind is justified in Christ—this is the fruit of His accomplished work—and also man is justified by faith alone. These two descriptions are not contradictory; both are scriptural and can be understood as non-contradictory, if we see the duality of justification—the two sides of reconciliation. Indeed, they reside in the closest relationship: there is no individual justification if justification is not first declared for the world. "Every proper argument for justification by faith is an argument for the objective justification which it necessarily presupposes, and every argument for objective justification is an argument for justification by faith as its proper goal and conclusion."[24] This is not dissimilar to the ways we may speak of salvation, redemption, and especially forgiveness.

The fact that the biblical terms overlap in meaning does not mean that they cannot be distinguished when approached from God's side and man's. The place the universality in Christ meets individuals is the Gospel. "In effect, viewed simply with respect to their final result, for sinful mankind, redemption, reconciliation, and justification can all be said to mean the same: the forgiveness of sins."[25] "In him we have redemption through his blood, the forgiveness of our trespasses, according to the riches of his grace" (Eph. 1:7). Redemption is synonymous with forgiveness, as is justification. Where the effects of Christ are stressed with no mention of faith, it does not automatically mean any one indi-

---

[23]Martin W. Diers, "Objective Justification: The Controversy Examined," 2013 Convocation of the Orthodox Lutheran Confessional Conference (http://lutherantheology.com/uploads/works/papers/ObjectiveJustification_2013_mwd.pdf), 9.

[24]Kurt Marquart, "Objective Justification," *Marquart's Works*, 6:98.

[25]Rick Curia, *History of Objective or Universal Justification*, 4.

vidual personally partakes of forgiveness without faith. On the other hand, the blood of Jesus is not made effective by faith. "For Walther and the Synodical Conference, the terminology of universal justification was introduced in order to defend the means of grace, especially absolution. They needed to explain why a pastor could forgive sins."[26] The objective aspect of the world's justification in Christ determines the very nature of forgiveness. It is the practical, tangible, publicly spoken forgiveness of the Gospel that is the touching point of man and God. This is the vital center of the justification debate in the modern era.

---

[26] Magnus Sørensen, "The Justification of Christ," 8.

Chapter 3

"Justification by Faith" is a Slogan

It is true that we are justified (individually) by faith, but this slogan is just that—a slogan, and not a full representation of the teaching of forgiveness in God's Word. In fact, this minimalistic stereotype leaves out the most important factor of justification: Christ and His work. However, for the modern deniers of objective justification—who claim that there is no aspect of, or basis for, justification before faith—this is said to be the only proper way to speak of justification: There is no "faithless, universal justification," because there can only be "one justification taught in Scripture—that of 'justification by grace through faith'."[1] It is a historically Lutheran way of speaking, though it has become an identifying phrase for Protestants in general. The issue is not the words themselves, but what they are used to say and avoid saying.

"In normal Biblical and ecclesiastical usage the terms 'justify' and 'justification' refer to the ('subjective') justification of the individual sinner through faith."[2] However, Satan does not rest, and false doctrine is not stagnant. We must be careful using 400-year-old phrases without

---

[1] Vernon H. Harley, "Synergism—Its Logical Association with General or Universal Justification" (1984; http://ichabodthegloryhasdeparted.blogspot.com/2015/12/synergism-its-logical-association-with.html).

[2] Commission on Theology and Church Relations, "Theses on Justification," The Lutheran Church–Missouri Synod (May, 1983; http://www.lcms.org/Document.fdoc?src=lcm&id=422), 8.

fully understanding what they were used to express and reject. We cannot rule out the possibility of a new error that hides behind traditional Lutheran slogans.

While the modern denial of objective justification says that objective justification is a new teaching, the reverse is actually true: the term is new, to be sure, but Christians are free to use any words to express the truth of God. There is no legalistic, ceremonial rule forbidding new terms or expanded meanings. The issue is whether the teaching, not the language, conforms to Scripture. It is the denial of objective justification that is new, though due to historical circumstances, it was not a teaching at the forefront until recently.

The concept expressed by objective justification is assumed and implicit in the understanding of pre-modern Lutherans because Scripture teaches an objective aspect to justification. It is the denial of the universal application and extent of Christ's redemptive work that is actually new.[3] While it may not have been expressed as distinctly and with the precise vocabulary of more modern Lutherans, the errors then were not such that doctrinal presentations required it. Lutherans have always understood that the forgiveness of sins and God's reconciliation—the appeasement of His wrath in Christ—are objective realities for the totality of mankind. Since this was not a matter of major disagreement, we should not expect to find clear statements addressing this contemporary heresy. In actuality, this objective aspect of salvation undergirds every dissemination of the Gospel. The issue is not the technical expression of objective justification, but the foundational basis of the Gospel it describes, which defines forgiveness and its power for mankind.

"No dogmatic formulation has absolute value."[4] Scripture establishes doctrine, not our limited understanding or human attempts at summa-

---

[3]Even classical Calvinists hold to an objective reconciliation, according to 2 Cor. 5:19, but only for the elect. "In discussing justification Calvin sometimes seems to conflate justification with the idea of reconciliation. For example, with reference to 2 Corinthians 5:21, he states of Paul: 'Doubtless, he means by the word "reconciled" nothing by justified' (Inst. III,11,4). I take 'reconciliation to pertain mainly to the objective aspect of the salvation accomplished for us by Christ' (2 Cor. 5:19). . . . In fact, like everything pertaining to salvation in Christ, justification can be seen to have both an objective and a subjective aspect." George Hunsinger, *Evangelical, Catholic, and Reformed: Doctrinal Essays on Barth and Related Themes* (Grand Rapids: Eerdmans, 2015), chapter 12, par. 5.

[4]Martin Franzmann, "Reconciliation and Justification," 83.

rizing its truth. All parts of the divine Word fit together into a dogmatic whole. We may not select only certain parts of the Bible, or even a majority of it, to fit into a certain system. Doctrine is singular and revealed, not logically derived, but we emphasize certain aspects more strongly in response to satanic errors, which usually try to take cover behind the bare text of Scripture.

In this issue of justification and its basis, various wordings and definitions may be profitably used. However, the rubber meets the road in the way the Gospel is actually used. Is the Gospel the application of forgiveness itself based on Christ's payment for sin and especially His resurrection? Or is the Gospel a sign post to tell sinners where forgiveness may be obtained? If the latter is true, forgiveness of sins, which overlaps with the definition of justification, is not delivered in the Word and is not an immediate consequence of Christ's work.

The theological roles of faith and Christ's resurrection are predicated on the teaching that has recently been termed "objective justification." The most practical and visible consequence of this debate is: In what sense may we tell anyone in the world (believer or non-believer) that they are forgiven, thereby actually forgiving their sins before God in heaven? This is extremely important to know, because if this justification—God's declaration that He is reconciled to mankind and forgives sins in Christ— is false, no one may be forgiven absolutely. The faith of a particular person is always in doubt from the viewpoint of sinners, but forgiveness is not a mere possibility to our Lord, in whom all are righteous.

Classic formulas may be helpful, but simple stereotypes of the divine truth based on the repetition of old slogans do not make for a full-bodied doctrine. No human phrasing can give the final word; Scripture, however, does. The most vocal denier of objective justification today falsely claims: "new terms and meanings must come from outside, alien to the long line of faithful gospel teachers."[5] Creeds, which are not simply repetitions of Bible verses, demarcate the truth from error. Heresy has always required new ways of confessing the truth and highlighting error. Another denier of objective justification from ELDoNA asserts: "what is at the very root of what our [2013 justification] theses . . . [is] a stripping away of false philosophical propositions."[6] In reality, we must

---

[5] Gregory Jackson, *Luther versus the Pietists*, 45.

[6] Eric Stefanski, "Theses on the Article of Justification: A Refutation of the ACLC's

use new terms when error claims the biblical vocabulary, as Christians have always done. Avoiding certain words, and their applicability to the Scripture's meaning, is needlessly restrictive. Claiming that every facet of justification is tied to faith, because of the slogan "faith alone," is a new error.

The scriptural faith versus works distinction, in regards to man's justification, is generally accepted by Protestants: "For we hold that one is justified by faith apart from works of the law" (Rom. 3:28). But the word "faith," by itself, even with the word "alone" added to it, does not preserve the true Gospel. Faith is truly taught and understood as a work (in biblical terms as something God demands in order to be satisfied with man) for most of Protestantism. So man's faith must be shown and confessed that it is not the effective power of Christ's work, but merely the reception of it. Faith does not create or make forgiveness, but appropriates what is already objectively there. This is the aim and motive of the increased emphasis on the objective aspect of justification.

"Justification by faith" is the battle cry of many who claim there is no justification without man's participation by faith. In a very helpful quote, an old Lutheran dogmatician elucidates the absoluteness of "faith" language:

> When it is said concerning faith, in the nominative case [as the subject] that IT justifies, the language seems to be figurative. The meaning is not that faith absolves a man from sins and accounts him righteous, but faith is said to justify, because God, in view of it, regards us righteous, or because faith (not by its own, but by the worth of Christ's merit) moves God to justify us.[7]

In a similar vein:

> Osiander justly remarks: "If we wish to speak accurately and according to Scripture, it must be said that God alone justifies (for it is an act of God alone); but by faith man is justified." For faith of itself does not justify, because it is merely apprehensive. The mode of speaking, because it has become so common to say, faith alone justifies, can be

Critique: Part Nine" (http://www.eldona.org/theses-on-the-article-of-justification-a-refutation-of-the-aclcs-critique-part-nine).

[7]Johannes Musaeus (1613–1681), quoted in: Heinrich Schmid, *The Doctrinal Theology of the Evangelical Lutheran Church,* trans. Charles A. Hay and Henry E. Jacobs (Minneapolis: Augsburg, 1875; reprint, Philadelphia: United Lutheran Publishing, 1961), 440.

retained, if the phrase be properly explained in accordance with Scripture usage.[8]

While it is perfectly fine to say that "faith saves," as Jesus Himself did, that is not the whole picture of salvation. A phrase is not equivalent to the revealed teaching of God, or a proper understanding of it. Justification is, properly, an act of God—a verdict over man. Where faith plays a larger role and overtakes the objective side of redemption, repeating a phrase proves nothing. Citing passages and quotes about faith's role does not illuminate God's role in what faith receives. This is a common plague among the deniers of any sort of objective justification.

"Faith alone" does not mean without Christ's death and suffering, God's grace, or the Word and sacraments. Faith is not an all-encompassing thing, outside of which there is no gracious God or historic resurrection of Christ—"faith alone" means salvation by Christ, without works of the law; it excludes man's works and efforts. But the word "faith," today, for most church bodies and traditions, does not do that. Faith is now the prime work done to merit and earn forgiveness. It is used in an entirely different sense than the Lutheran reformers used it.

The stress on objective justification safeguards the basis of justification. It shows that justification is not because of man, or caused by man, in any way. If faith effects justification and is a condition that must be met for God to be forgiving toward man, it is a work of the law, plain and simple. Faith would then be a requirement of the law, as something man must do, because justification is not directly dependent on Christ's work. This is the role of faith in conversion for many Protestant churches. In contrast, the old Lutheran teaching of faith is quite limited—it has no meritorious value to God: "Faith alone justifies; that is, it is the only organ by which we lay hold of the righteousness of Christ and apply it to ourselves."[9] The righteousness of Christ is not completed by faith, but it lies ready-made in the Gospel, since the world was forgiven in Christ.

In this dual nature of forgiveness, each aspect must be presented in

---

[8] Andreas Osiander (1498–1552), quoted in: Heinrich Schmid, *The Doctrinal Theology of the Evangelical Lutheran Church*, 440.

[9] Johannes Andreas Quenstedt (1617–1688), quoted in: Heinrich Schmid, *The Doctrinal Theology of the Evangelical Lutheran Church*, 440.

accordance with Scripture.

> Of the instrumental causes [of justification] there are again
> two kinds, the one kind from God's side, the other from the
> side of man. From God's side they are Word and Sacrament.
> And here all parties already diverge. From the side of man
> it is faith, and here there is a truly Babylonian confusion
> among the sects, when it comes to the point of explaining
> what faith is.[10]

While this duality of justification is not easily formulated into a digestible
slogan, the divine truth calls us to preserve the freedom that exists in
Christ, which is constantly under attack from "false brothers secretly
brought in—who slipped in to spy out our freedom that we have in
Christ Jesus, so that they might bring us into slavery" (Gal. 2.4). Satan
hates the freedom found in Christ and His Gospel, and so seeks to
enslave by the law and accursed works. It is all the better for the devil
if the Gospel word "faith" becomes a celebrated work to propitiate a
still angry god, so no one is freed by the preaching of this "faith."

---

[10]Walther, *Justification—Objective and Subjective*, 8.

Chapter 4

Limiting the Debate

Like most intra-family squabbles, the debate over justification has been hostile, bitter, and unsympathetic. At times it has been more a battle of words, instead of what Scripture teaches concerning the Gospel. This modern debate has frequently been used as a tool to attack certain church bodies, because to attack one's teaching of justification is to disparage the core of one's Lutheran identity. Bitter words and uncharitable logical extensions of the other's position have dominated the debate. Twisting what the other side is actually saying has been prevalent in this issue. The two sides just cannot see where the other is coming from, because they operate with different theological frameworks.

A key error on both sides of the debate is making conclusions and logical inferences for the other party that they themselves did not make. The same was true of the earlier absolution controversy of the late 1800s, which dealt with the same underlying issues of the nature of forgiveness and the extent of justification: "The Augustana Synod [which denied objective justification] men tried to credit the Norwegian Synod [which upheld objective justification] with statements and conclusions they have never made, nor intended to make."[1] Charges of universalism, that all must be saved if all are justified in Christ, have been a constant refrain, despite the fact that no actual statement is shown to have this conclusion. It is a rational extension by the opposing party, rather than a confessed position.

---

[1] Rick Curia, *History of Objective or Universal Justification*, 21.

26

Instead, universalism has been universally denied—which made the deniers of a universal justification all the more suspicious. In the 1870's, "August Weenaas and Sven Ofterdahl, two of the professors on the faculty of Augsburg, accused the Norwegian Synod, and H. A. Preus in particular, of universalism."[2] In the 1980s it was said: "The first of such implications [of objective justification] is an unscriptural universalism."[3] Citing Rom. 8:30, "whom He justified, these He also glorified," it is assumed justification can only mean one thing and have only one aspect. "In other words, to make justification universal, one must either eliminate a major portion of this and many other passages of Scripture or one must teach universal final salvation."[4] Those who teach objective justification are said to "love terms that convey God's universalism, which is utterly contrary to the Scriptures."[5]

The universalist suspicion, which is denied by orthodox Lutherans who hold to an objective justification in Christ, depends on human logic and a false misunderstanding of intent. While it may sound like two separate and disparate justifications are intended, this is rather a fine distinction in the one matter of justification to show its foundation in Christ.

> Justification is both objective and subjective, yet it is not two doctrines or two justifications, but rather one justification that is accomplished objectively and universally and distributed and appropriated subjectively and individually. We do not separate the doctrine of justification into two separate species, one which is apart from faith ("faithless justification"), and the other that includes faith. The distinction of universal and individual within the doctrine of justification is a distinction within one substance.[6]

On the other side, it is assumed: "Scripture teaches only one justification; namely, the one by faith in Christ, Romans 3:28."[7] The use of reason

---

[2]Martin Diers, "Objective Justification," 3.

[3]Vernon Harley, "Synergism—Its Logical Association with General Justification."

[4]Vernon Harley, "Synergism—Its Logical Association with General Justification."

[5]Gregory Jackson, "Some Clarity about Objective Justification *versus* the Chief Article" (Nov. 13, 2018; http://ichabodthegloryhasdeparted.blogspot.com/2018/11/some-clarity-about-objective.html).

[6]Jon Buchholz, "Jesus Canceled Your Debt!," 1.

[7]Walter A. Maier [II], "A Summary Exposition of the Doctrine of Justification by Grace Through Faith" (1981; http://www.wlsessays.net/bitstream/handle/123456789/3210/MaierJustification.pdf), 17.

and the validity of logical extensions is a massive part of this debate.

Another sticking point in this justification debate among Lutherans has been denominational pride. The LCMS has been the focal point of attacks on the teaching of justification intermittently since the late 1800s. Interestingly enough, ELDoNA is now playing the part of the more doctrinally liberal synods from the late 1800s to the mid-1900s—when they stopped caring about doctrine at all. It is said of a theologian in 1871 that perhaps he "simply wanted to use this controversy as an opportunity to take some shots at the Missouri Synod" by calling objective justification "The Missouri-Norwegian doctrine." This led to a later charge of universalism by the same theologian: "The Missouri-Norwegian doctrine teaches that each godless person is justified, has received the forgiveness of sins; and is (objectively) a child of God."[8] Despite the fact that Missouri did not actually teach those conclusions, it was an easy charge to make without actually considering their position.

This disagreement in justification became the club used to dole out synodical abuse, as R.C.H. Lenski, of commentary fame, did later. It is said of him that "The implication [Lenski makes] is, if we follow the line of argument, that the Missourians of necessity must represent God as preaching the Gospel in hell."[9] Observe what could be an inflammatory blog post today, but comes from 1888:

> One must ask himself with astonishment, how one is to explain that the hundreds of these pastors, following as pilgrims, true to their leader, allowed themselves to remain mute and silent, when, for them, *justification was moved out of the doctrine of justification; the doctrine of justification was thrown out of the third article;* the heart of the doctrine of justification (the *actus forensis* [forensic act]) was taken out; the bare shell (the act of men, the reception, the personal comfort) alone was allowed to remain: and when, thus, the Lutheran concept of justification was abandoned—in fact, was damned as false doctrine![10]

---

[8]George Fritschel, quoted in: Rick Curia, *History of Objective or Universal Justification*, 30–31, 32.

[9]Theodore Engelder (1865–1949), quoted in: Rick Curia, *History of Objective or Universal Justification*, 33.

[10]Gottfried Fritschel, quoted in: Rick Curia, *History of Objective or Universal Justification*, 52.

ELDoNA has now made the denial of objective justification their identifying mark, even going so far as to release a documentary warning people about its dangers.[11] Strangely enough, almost all ELDoNA pastors confessed it themselves implicitly by spending years in synods which confessed objective justification, without saying a word against it. The main issue is not the inference of universalism, though it makes for a winsome soundbite:

> It is our unanimous understanding that salvation is received by the individual sinner only through faith, that none are to be regarded as saved except through faith. . . . We condemn every form of universalism and any thought that Man has the merit and righteousness of Christ applied to him other than through that faith. . . . [12]

The bone of contention is actually the use of reason in interpreting Scripture:

> It is absurd to imagine that Paul was talking about "our justification" in 4:25 as an objective justification that was pronounced upon all people not by faith, and then immediately changed the discussion in the very next verse to refer to "our justification" ("we, having been justified,") as a completely separate event (i.e., subjective justification), without any such indication in the text.[13]

Ruling out the possibility of a universal aspect to justification, due to its affront to reason, ELDoNA cannot consider the objective and subjective aspects harmoniously coexisting. But Christian theologians have always transitioned between both the subjective and objective aspects seamlessly—as Scripture itself does. The nuanced scriptural import is overrun by the overreaching conclusions of reason, which refuses to acknowledge "this absurdity that God has already declared all people righteous whether they believe in the Righteous One or not."[14]

One of the understated issues in this long-standing dialogue is not just the use of Scripture, but its clarity. In the ELDoNA theses against

---

[11]Youtube documentary, "Justification Made Clear," Parts 1-9 (2018; http://www.youtube.com/watch?v=7HJs5sbAnyo).

[12]ELDoNA, "Theses on the Article of Justification," 2–3.

[13]Paul Rydecki, "On Francis Pieper's Misuse of Romans 4:25 as a Biblical Basis for Objective Justification," Colloquium of the Evangelical Lutheran Diocese of North America, Fort Wayne, IN (Jan. 16, 2018; http://www.godwithuslc.org/wp-content/uploads/2018/02/On-Pieper-and-Romans-4_2017.pdf), 15.

[14]Letter from Rydecki to President Jon Buchholz.

objective justification, Scripture is minimized and made to be unclear, as if it is without a plain and simple meaning inspired by the Spirit. "We must distinguish between what a passage could, conceivably, mean, what it most probably means, and what it must mean."[15] This is perhaps the most egregious statement in the ELDoNA Theses. Sinful reason does not want to be bound by Scripture. Instead it wants to make it simplistic and without difficulties. Verses that are unclear to sinful man, are said to be less authoritative in practice. This is an illegitimate use of reason. Reason, instead, must submit to God's Word, even where it sees a contradiction, or else the Word will be manhandled. We may not say that the Spirit, who inspired Scripture, was careless when He spoke of justification without mentioning faith, but more accurate in other passages where justification is linked closely to faith. Both the objective and subjective aspects of justification are part of the one truth God revealed through the Spirit's words. The substance of this issue is the Word of God and what doctrine it actually reveals to us, even if it does not jive with our preconceived notions. "Since Scripture teaches both facts [of justification] we let them stand side by side."[16]

Many of the charges and condemnations are personally injurious, unwarranted, and uncalled for. According to Scripture, we must not fight over words (2 Tim. 2:14). However, we must fight over the substance of what God has revealed of the mystery of Christ, so this issue, however distasteful the arguments, cannot be ignored. There is a real divide over the heart of the Gospel between these parties, and this cannot be an issue of no concern to those who love God's truth. Those who love Christ are to expose what is not of God, what is not given to us in Holy Scripture.

Most denials of objective justification get caught up in verbal legalism, legislating what may or may not be said. Then particular snippets assuming the objective aspect of justification are attacked with personal polemics, with very little actual instruction and elucidation of Scripture. Bound up with this verbal legalism is a stilted view of language and tradition. It is assumed that only old theological words of Lutheran provenance are valid, and they can only be used in the way they

---

[15]Thesis 15, ELDoNA, "Theses on the Article of Justification," 7.

[16]Franz Pieper, "C.F.W. Walther as Theologian: Justification, Universal," in *Lehre und Wehre* (Feb. 1890), trans. Wallace McLaughlin (http://backtoluther.blogspot.com/2013/02/walther-as-theologian-justification-by_28.html), 5.

have been used historically. For example: "the WELS [condemned] Pr. Rydecki for speaking the Gospel precisely as Lutherans during and after the Reformation did."[17] The problem with false doctrine is not just the phrasing and vocabulary, of course. Heresy routinely hides itself behind traditional slogans and orthodox innuendo.

Since it is solely Scripture's message that is at stake, there is no need to defend every use of the term "objective justification." It need only be shown that it can be defined and used in a scriptural way, so that it does not conflict with any other Christian teaching. The issue is not human phrasing, but rather the lustful eye of fleshly logic, which cannot submit to the bare Word of God. A denier of objective justification insinuates:

> Why preach the Gospel? If all men have already been justified, i.e., declared and accepted by God as righteous prior to and apart from faith, then logically there is no need for faith in order to be saved. Hence there is also no need for preaching the Gospel through which men are brought to faith.[18]

The counterpoint is that for forgiveness to be "seriously and efficaciously offered to all in the means of grace," it must exist before the effect of that gracious Word—faith.[19] The Gospel creates faith by forgiving sinners their sins, not by creating forgiveness in alchemic reaction with man's response to it.

The caricature, both old and new, is that a so-called "universal, objective justification" is a justification in the place of faith, ruling out that faith alone justifies. This bad logical inference denies implicitly any aspect of justification reaching back to Christ's work. It disconnects forgiveness from Christ. Faith alone does not mean there is forgiveness without Christ or His resurrection—far from it. The objective aspect of justification "is not the justification which we receive by faith, but the one which took place before all faith. In Christ we were justified before we were even born."[20] The universal side to justification gets to

---

[17]Eric Stefanski, "Theses on the Article of Justification: A Refutation of the ACLC's Critique: Part One."

[18]Vernon Harley, "Synergism—Its Logical Association with General Justification."

[19]CTCR, "Theses on Justification," 8.

[20]Edward Preuss, *Justification of the Sinner before God,* trans. J. A. Friedrich (*Concordia Theological Monthly,* 1928–29; reprint, Fort Wayne: Concordia Theological Seminary Press, 1970), 8.

the base and foundation of forgiveness—what faith itself actually relies on. This is not only a valid area of investigation, but a necessary one today.

We may go before "justification by faith" to its basis by asking the question: What makes forgiveness available and when did the basis for it occur? It has been correctly said that objective justification is not a substitute for faith, but rather that "it forms the basis of the justification by faith and keeps this article free from the leaven of Pelagianism."[21] The quarrel manifests itself not in technical distinctions, but the role of faith in relation to the Gospel: Does faith create forgiveness out of thin air by applying Christ's atonement in a propitiatory act, or is faith merely the empty hand that receives what the resurrected Christ gives out of the completion of His work, so that faith gets no credit for salvation or its acceptance?

The debate is not about the atonement, if it is strictly defined as payment for sin. Considered narrowly, in this way, the atonement has no effect—it does not do anything, insofar as mankind as a whole is concerned. "The vicarious satisfaction is thus limited to the pre-resurrection events."[22] The main question in this debate is what does Christ's resurrection, not His death, mean and give to mankind? For deniers of objective justification, forgiveness—the product of our Savior's justification—is outside the scope of Christ's earthly work. Forgiveness, for them, is only a present-tense reality. It is certainly something that occurs in time, but forgiveness depends on and flows from Christ's work, not man's reception of it. Forgiveness is received in faith, but it does not come from faith. So the dimension of objective justification is employed "in order to explain the import of Christ's satisfaction."[23]

The extent of the efficacy, or the results, of Christ's work is at the heart of this vocal clash. Scripture speaks to the judgment and pardon

---

[21]Theodore Engelder (1933), quoted in: Gregory Jackson, *Luther versus the Pietists*, 115.

[22]Tom G. A. Hardt, "Justification and Easter: A Study in Subjective and Objective Justification in Lutheran Theology," *A Lively Legacy: Essays in Honor of Robert Preus*, eds. Kurt E. Marquart, John R. Stephenson, and Bjarne W. Teigen (Fort Wayne: Concordia Theological Seminary Press, 1985; http://luk.se/Justification-Easter.htm), 53.

[23]F.A. Schmidt (1837–1923), quoted in: Rick Curia, *History of Objective or Universal Justification*, 26.

of sin as having a "sameness of their extension and universality."[24] "Therefore, as through one man's offense judgment came to all men, resulting in condemnation, even so through one Man's righteous act the free gift came to all men, resulting in justification of life." (Rom. 5:18; NKJV). But as all are not actually finally damned, but only those found solely in Adam, so all are justified in Christ, but not all come to Christ through faith. These universal judgments are not logical facts to be manipulated. From the side of Christ, justification is complete, but to take hold of these available benefits, from man's side, one must be in Christ, which occurs only through faith. So Christ not only won and created the possibility for forgiveness, He actually offers it to all men in the Gospel. Faith depends on forgiveness itself, not the promise of acceptance once certain conditions are met.

The two sentences and judgments, one in Adam and one in Christ, are simultaneously in effect. One is not stronger or more valid than the other. Christ's act of righteousness is not less effective than Adam's original sin. One does not cancel the other: "so that as sin reigned in death, even so grace might reign through righteousness to eternal life through Jesus Christ our Lord" (Rom. 5:21). Of course, the ways the verdicts come to us and are grasped are vastly different: one we are born into, and the other comes in the Gospel promise. Both the extent and potency of these universal declarations are at the crux of the objective justification debate—God's twin verdicts, which are often stylized as simply law and Gospel.

---

[24]F.A. Schmidt, quoted in: Rick Curia, *History of Objective or Universal Justification*, 27.

Chapter 5

Defining Forgiveness

While the terms and definitions of objective and subjective justification are somewhat abstract and foreign to many, the root of this distinction is the forgiveness of sins. Justification is one synonym of forgiveness, though it usually refers to the personal reception of that absolution. "To attain the remission of sins is to be justified, according to Ps. 32:1" (*Apology to the Augsburg Confession* [Ap] 4:76). Objective justification does not refer to a secret, hidden declaration, but what actually happened to Christ, and is present in the Gospel. This general aspect to justification directly determines the forgiveness of sins, which is not created by man or faith. Justification, having the root in Greek meaning "righteous," can be used to speak of righteousness in several ways. As a direct product of Christ's work, "Justification is first the non-imputation of our sins or the 'forgiveness of sins'."[1] This wider definition is applicable to the "world," according to Scripture: "God was in Christ reconciling the world to Himself, not imputing their trespasses to them" (2 Cor. 5:19).

Absolution is often defined as the declaration of forgiveness, the removal of sins before God, not its positive reception by man. This gets to the center of objective justification, which determines the inherent power of the forgiving Word. There are three passages of Scripture in which Christ directly gives the power to forgive, and not merely the potential for sins to be forgiven at a later time. It was said to Peter: "I

---

[1]Martim C. Warth, "Justification through Faith in Article Four of the Apology," *CTQ* 46:2–3 (April–July 1982; http://www.ctsfw.net/media/pdfs/warthjustification.pdf), 118.

will give you the keys of the kingdom of heaven, and whatever you bind on earth shall be bound in heaven, and whatever you loose on earth shall be loosed in heaven" (Matt. 16:19). To the apostles Jesus said: "If you forgive the sins of any, they are forgiven them; if you withhold forgiveness from any, it is withheld" (Jn. 20:23). Of the three passages instituting the power of the keys—the ability given to man to unlock or lock heaven to a sinner—Luther used Matt. 18:18 the most, because its context includes every Christian, not merely a subset as in the other two passages. "Truly, I say to you, whatever you bind on earth shall be bound in heaven, and whatever you loose on earth shall be loosed in heaven" (Matt. 18:18).

The definition of the Gospel specifically as an absolution, as forgiveness itself, is a Lutheran teaching.

> The preaching of the holy gospel itself is principally and actually an absolution in which forgiveness of sins is proclaimed in general and in public to many persons, or publicly or privately to one person alone. Therefore absolution may be used in public and in general, and in special cases also in private, just as the sermon may take place publicly or privately, and as one might comfort many people in public or someone individually in private. Even if not all believe [the word of absolution], that is no reason to reject [public] absolution, for each absolution, whether administered publicly or privately, has to be understood as demanding faith and as being an aid to those who believe in it, just as the gospel itself also proclaims forgiveness to all men in the whole world and exempts no one from this universal context. Nevertheless the gospel certainly demands our faith and does not aid those who do not believe it; and yet the universal context of the gospel has to remain [valid].[2]

Defining the Gospel as real and actual forgiveness means that it is not a ceremonial rite of man, but the power that Christ merited and gave, and which therefore, belongs to every baptized Christian. This identification of forgiveness with the Gospel is only possible because the universal character of Christ's atonement changed "the relation in which the world stands to God as far as it no longer remains the object

---

[2]Martin Luther and Philip Melanchthon, "Letter to the Council of the City of Nürnberg" (1533), *Luther's Works,* eds. Jaroslav Pelikan and Helmut Lehmann, 56 vols. (St. Louis: Concordia Publishing House; Philadelphia: Fortress Press, 1955–86), 50:76–77.

of His wrath."[3] In a very real sense, the world has been absolved in Christ. Luther speaks of sin being universally removed in Christ: "If Christ Himself is made guilty of all the sins that we have all committed, then we are absolved from all sins, not through ourselves or through our own works or merits but through Him."[4]

From God's perspective, any absolution is valid because all have been absolved in Christ's resurrection.[5] Whatever absolution is delivered, "that absolution is not based on the state of man's heart, but entirely on the state of" God, who forgives.[6] Therefore, a pastor should be continually absolving when administering the Gospel. There is no true Gospel without a corresponding release from sins, whether it is spoken of exactly in these terms or not. This power is not to be hidden under a bushel. The Lutheran Confessions state in the *Treatise on the Power and Primacy of the Pope:* "Thus [Christ] grants the power of the keys principally and without mediation to the church, and for the same reason the church has primary possession of the right to call ministers" (23). Luther could speak of the reality of sin universally wiped out, without mentioning faith at all:

> By this deed the whole world is purged and expiated from all sins, and thus it is set free from death and from every evil. But when sin and death have been abolished by this one man, God does not want to see anything else in the whole world, especially if it were to believe, except sheer cleansing and righteousness. And if any remnants of sin were to remain, still for the sake of Christ, the shining Sun, God would not notice them.[7]

The war over justification in the modern Lutheran church is really a battle for the basis of forgiveness and to whom the Gospel absolution applies:

> Then the Romanizing doctrine of some Lutherans on absolution as an exclusive right of ordained pastors, according to which lay absolution has but little or no significance, and as

---

[3]Conrad Emil Lindberg, *Christian Dogmatics and Notes on the History of Dogma,* trans. C. E. Hoffsten (Rock Island, IL: Augustana Book Concern, 1922), 260.

[4]"Lectures on Galatians" (1535), LW 26:280.

[5]C. F. W. Walther, *Essays for the Church,* 2 vols. (St. Louis: Concordia Publishing House, 1992), 1:234.

[6]Francis Pieper, *Christian Dogmatics,* 4 vols., trans. T. Engelder, J. T. Mueller and W. W. F. Albrecht (St. Louis: Concordia Publishing House, 1953), 3:195.

[7]"Lectures on Galatians" (1535), LW 26:280.

declared to be only a comforting encouragement without a real communication of the forgiveness of sins itself, is grossly in conflict with the doctrine of the immediate power of God's Word and the Holy Sacraments. And this, to an alarming extent, destroys the sinner's full comfort as it is found in the doctrine of absolution, which is the power to forgive sins, which is given to the whole Christian Church on earth, and hence to each individual in it.[8]

This confession of the "real communication of the forgiveness of sins itself," depends on the teaching of objective justification. The comfort of the Gospel as a true absolution depends on forgiveness being a done deal. The stakes are high.

The keys, as summarized in the fifth chief part of the Small Catechism, are a power to use. "Confession has two parts. First, that we confess our sins, and second, that we receive absolution, that is, forgiveness, from the pastor as from God Himself, not doubting, but firmly believing that by it our sins are forgiven before God in heaven." Forgiveness is available to all. The Gospel is not a mere instruction manual, telling where or how forgiveness may be obtained, but a true unlocking. Every use of the Gospel is an absolution itself by God in heaven, or else it is not the Gospel. "Absolution is the forgiveness of sins, which is the sum and substance of the Holy Gospel itself."[9] So every use of the Gospel is a true absolution, an unlocking of heaven. But the Gospel is not particular; it is not just for certain people. It is universal (Matt. 28:19). Christ gave this "power of God for salvation" (Rom. 1:16) in the Gospel, "an absolution, addressed to the whole world."[10]

What is the source and foundation of forgiveness, and therefore the Gospel? Not faith, but Christ and His salvific work. "Consequently, there must lie hidden in the keys of Christ his blood, death, and resurrection, by which he has opened to us heaven, and thus imparts through the keys to poor sinners what he has wrought through his blood."[11] This word, "impart," speaks of what the keys give. "The loosing key [which forgives] flows out from the objective forgiveness of all for whom Jesus

---

[8] John Humberger, *Absolution; or Forgiveness of Sins: Established by the Holy Scriptures,* Tract. No. 5 (Columbus, OH: Lutheran Book Concern, 1880; reprint, Omaha, NE: Mercinator Press, 2019), 2.

[9] John Humberger, *Absolution*, 1.

[10] F. Pieper, *Christian Dogmatics*, 3:197.

[11] Luther, "The Keys" (1530), LW 40:328.

died, and announces that forgiveness to everyone who now hears the spoken word of absolution."[12] Justification of the individual, the actual reception and taking hold of forgiveness in faith, "can only happen because . . . forgiveness already exists in Christ and is objectively conferred in absolution as in the gospel."[13]

Luther underlined the role of the absolving Gospel, in all its forms, in creating and sustaining faith:

> And we must have many absolutions, so that we may strengthen our timid consciences and despairing hearts against the devil and against God. . . . For our God is not so miserly that He has left us with only one comfort or strengthening for our conscience, or one absolution, but we have many absolutions in the Gospel, and are showered richly with them. For instance, we have this in the Gospel: "If ye forgive men their trespasses, your heavenly Father will also forgive you" (Matt. 6:14). Another comfort we have in the Lord's Prayer: "Forgive us our trespasses," etc (Matt. 6:12). A third is our baptism, when I reason thus: See, my Lord, I am baptized in Thy name so that I may be assured of Thy grace and mercy. After that we have the private confession, when I go and receive a sure absolution as if God Himself spake it, so that I may be assured that my sins are forgiven. Finally I take to myself the blessed sacrament, when I eat His body and drink His blood as a sign that I am rid of my sins and God has freed me from all my frailties; and in order to make me sure of this, He gives me His body to eat and His blood to drink, so that I shall not and cannot despair: I cannot doubt I have a gracious God.[14]

The Gospel, as explained by the keys to heaven Christ gave, is an active power, but more than that, it is a universal verdict. It not only describes and tells about the forgiveness Christ won, it actually delivers and imparts it. This explains how Luther can call the "mutual conversation and consolation of the brothers" a private use of the Gospel,

---

[12]David Jay Webber, "Our Righteousness before God . . . is Revealed in the Gospel. On this Righteousness Faith Relies," The Emmaus Conference, Tacoma, Washington (April 22-23, 2015; http://www.angelfire.com/ny4/djw/WebberEmmausConferenceEssay.pdf), 40.

[13]Magnus Sørensen, "The Justification of Christ," 35.

[14]Martin Luther, "The Eighth Sermon: A Short Summary of The Sermon of Dr. M. Luther Delivered on Reminiscere Sunday on Private Confession," in *The Works of Martin Luther* (Philadelphia: A. J. Holman, 1915; http://www.godrules.net/library/luther/NEW1luther_b8.htm), 422–25; Also translated in LW 51:97–100.

on par with the power of public preaching.[15] Though Christ died for all, not all receive and possess redemption. The benefits of His resurrection are distributed in the promise of the Gospel and received in faith. Faith is not needed to complete salvation, for all sinners are already justified in Christ's rising. "Christ has redeemed *all,* and merited remission of sins for *all* without exception."[16] This is an unconditional Gospel—an effective Gospel that delivers its content, the forgiveness of sins. "Only if justification depends entirely on Christ and His works, can salvation be by grace alone."[17]

In a 1533 sermon on Matthew 9:1–8, the healing of the paralytic, Luther states:

> Such power [to forgive sins] began, as we hear in this account, with Christ himself, and it continues for mankind, especially with those who occupy the pastoral office and are duty bound to preach repentance and the forgiveness of sins in Jesus' name. Nevertheless, every Christian has the command, not only that he can, but should, say to you when you are troubled by your sin: Why are you troubled? As your fellow Christian, I say to you, you are not fair to yourself, for God is not ungracious toward you; you ought to trust these words just as surely as though God were speaking to you personally from heaven, never questioning them because of the person of the one from whom you hear them.[18]

An individual can only be forgiven because the world has already been forgiven in Christ, who bore the guilt of the world. "When the pastor now absolves, he distributes a treasure which already exists, namely the forgiveness of sins already acquired."[19] Forgiveness is not an abstract

---

[15]The entire article reads: "We will now return to the Gospel, which not merely in one way gives us counsel and aid against sin; for God is superabundantly rich in His grace. First, through the spoken Word by which the forgiveness of sins is preached in the whole world; which is the peculiar office of the Gospel. Secondly, through Baptism. Thirdly, through the holy Sacrament of the Altar. Fourthly, through the power of the keys, and also through the mutual conversation and consolation of brethren, Matt. 18:20: Where two or three are gathered together, etc." *Smalcald Articles* III, 4.

[16]E. Hove, *Christian Doctrine* (Minneapolis: Augsburg, 1930), 226.

[17]Walther, *Justification—Objective and Subjective,* 42.

[18]Martin Luther, *Complete Sermons of Martin Luther,* 7 vols., eds. John Nicholas Lenker and Eugene F. A. Klug (Grand Rapids: Baker Books, 2000; vol. 1–4 published as *Sermons of Martin Luther: The Church Postils,* 8 vols. in 4 vols., 1995; vols. 5–7 published as *Sermons of Martin Luther: The House Postils,* 3 vols. 1996), 7:79–80.

[19]Walther, *Justification—Objective and Subjective,* 20.

idea, but what is preached and communicated.

> Forgiveness is a real sending off of sin. And whenever we talk about forgiveness *before* God, we are talking about a real act, or real acts, *of* God. The forgiveness that Jesus won for us is not a pile of inanimate supernatural "stuff" that has been made available to God by the work of Christ, so that he can, as needed, scoop up some of it and pass it out to people. The forgiveness that we preach is, rather, a forgiveness that was established as an ongoing, vibrant reality for all people, by two closely related 'sendings off' of sin.[20]

Consider this explanation of Jn. 1:29, by a denier of objective justification, that disconnects Christ's accomplished work from forgiveness:

> This is a beautiful passage that you have corrupted to force it to say more than it says. It speaks clearly about the universality of Christ's sacrifice, but it says not a word about the application of Christ's sacrifice to the world, as if all men had already been forgiven or justified on account of it. Christ surely bore the sin of the world and suffered for the sin of the world, and so has merited or earned forgiveness of sins for all people. "By His death, Christ made satisfaction for our sins" (*Augsburg Confession* 4). Therefore, John the Baptist rightly directs his disciples to "behold" the Lamb of God, that they might become partakers through faith in the forgiveness of sins that He merited for all (or, at that time, would merit) through His sacrifice.[21]

The word "world" is twisted to mean just "believers" and "take away" to mean "might be taken away, if faith is added." Forgiveness is about more than the payment Christ made—it is the effect of Christ's work, the application and acceptance of Christ's death for man. A forgiveness that is not applicable universally is not something that can be received or believed.

That Jesus died for forgiveness is a large part of the Gospel, but Jesus did not stay dead. Sin did not win. The world's reconciliation is a direct effect of the atonement, or an essential part of it.

> At the 1860 [Missouri Synod] convention, it was also confessed that this universal justification was a representative justification: "As surely as Christ has died, and died for all people, so surely God sees all people as dead for the sake of their sins. Christ's death has redeemed . . . as [a] death for

---

[20]David Jay Webber, "Our Righteousness before God," 46.
[21]Letter from Rydecki to President Jon Buchholz.

all people. On the other hand, Christ is also raised in the stead of all people, thus all people are declared righteous in Christ; for Christ needed to be as the Righteous One for His person not by resurrection, but this has been done for our sake, He died and rose again in their place, and thus all are justified in Christ."[22]

The resurrection, as with justification, is the oft neglected link between Christ's death and the believer's faith—and this doctrinal connection indicates the nature of the Gospel, the forgiveness of sins which saves before God.

---

[22]Quoted in: Magnus Sørensen, "The Justification of Christ," 6.

Chapter 6

A Modern Gospel in which Faith Replaces Christ

The Gospel is not simply an if/then conditional statement: where if man gives God faith, then, and only then, will God forgive him. The Reformers were careful to avoid this, but they were dealing with a different doctrinal error: the reception of forgiveness by the individual was said to be by a combination of works and faith. The error is much more subtle in modern Lutheranism.

Neither is the issue—at least among Lutherans who take their Confessions seriously—about whether faith is man-made or God-given. Both sides acknowledge that faith is worked by the Spirit in the Word and given as a gift. Both sides agree in principle to how faith comes. The contrast is in the application of the Gospel: Can you tell any sinner he is forgiven in Christ? This very practical question is not about who should actually be forgiven at a particular point in time—the unrepentant may not be forgiven, since they are ruled by sin and have no desire for grace. No, that would lead to greater sin, since they already despise the forgiving absolution of the Gospel. This question instead delves into whom the Gospel is directed at and valid for.

The very efficacy or effect of the Gospel is the real point of disagreement. If the Gospel demands something, it does not merely give forgiveness and absolve of its own power. If justification is conditional upon faith, and not a consequence of Christ's resurrection, the Gospel cannot be the forgiveness of sins itself. It may be a pointer to it, but it cannot objectively communicate the verdict of God. This presents a conundrum, since the Gospel, properly defined, is the forgiveness of sins that gives rise to faith.

This error of basing justification on faith effectively leaves a gap between Christ's payment for sin and the results of the Father's acceptance of that payment. If it happens in faith, the Gospel is not the "power of God," as God declares that it is; rather, it is powerless information, confronting the sinner with a choice: to believe and win God's favor or fail to meet its stated terms and leave the potential offer unfulfilled. The Gospel then morphs into powerless if/then conditional statements, making faith the prerequisite to God's forgiving relationship to the world, drastically changing the nature of preaching and what is actually said from the pulpit. Forgiveness, without an objective basis, becomes a distant abstraction, not an ever-present reality onto which faith latches. To answer the question "What is the Gospel?" we must have a position on the meaning of "objective justification," even if we choose not to use these words.

If the objective dimension to justification is rejected, then the "forgiveness of sins and justification for all have not been declared by God when He raised His Son from the dead, but have merely been acquired or made a possibility through Christ's atonement."[1] Without a real declaration, there is no forgiveness, since forgiveness itself is a verdict of righteousness spoken by the Father for the sake of Christ.

However, there is another difficulty, which makes this issue of objective justification somewhat of a tangled mess, from a human standpoint. Not all that is called objective justification is what 19th century Lutherans confessed as their teaching. An unbiblical overemphasis on this teaching, and a causal, careless speaking of it, developed in the 20th century—so that justification was applied to individuals outside of Christ. This undue widening of the understanding of objective justification is just as dangerous as the denial of it, and in itself can derail and deform the one true Gospel of Christ.

Just like justification by faith, objective justification can become a mantra, and destructive hammer, when used without true biblical

---

[1]CTCR, "Theses on Justification," 12.

understanding. "It is evident how diligent the devil is to cheat Lutheran Christians out of the palladium [the source of protection] of their confession, the true doctrine of justification, with Lutheran-sounding formulas and flowery phrases."[2] And, unfortunately, both "objective justification" and "justification by faith" have been used to cause confusion, whether purposely or through careless, sloppy wording.

However, this more recent abuse of objective justification does not detract from the truth of a general justification of mankind in Christ—as the theological saying goes: the abuse of a thing does not take away its proper use. We must be careful not to overreact to an overreaction—and end up twice as wrong.

In the earliest theological controversies, as with all hard-fought doctrinal battles, the resulting creeds and confessions used new words and phrases, which had to be carefully defined and refined over many years. So it is with this debate over the Gospel and its relation to justification. There have been at least 150 years of divisive disputes among Lutherans in several parts of the world, as "The doctrine of general justification was a matter of some dispute in the Finnish Lutheran Church at the turn of the 19th century." In that particular altercation, an 1880 document expressed that "it was precisely Christ's resurrection that effected [mankind's] general justification."[3] This bitter fight is truly about the essence of Lutheran identity, because those who are unscriptural on justification have lost any right to bear the name "Lutheran."

---

[2] George Stoeckhardt, "General Justification," 140.

[3] *Encyclopedia of Martin Luther and the Reformation,* vol. 2, ed. Mark A. Lamport (Lanham, MD: Rowman and Littlefield, 2017), 279–80.

Chapter 7

False Implications

Some deniers of objective justification have made inflammatory assumptions without cause or basis, which shows how divisive this issue is. "Champions of [objective justification] rail against faith, belittling faith, mocking faith, as if it were bad, dangerous, and a work of man."[1] Objective justification has been called a "strange concoction of double justification, grace without means, forgiveness without the Word, without faith," but this position fails to see the dual nature of justification.[2]

If the answer is to be clear-cut and justification entirely one-sided, one aspect of justification must be eliminated: "The main question is: are the entire world's sins forgiven or are they not?"[3] Scripture clearly states that, from God's side, yes, sins are forgiven—when considering the world in Christ. Without faith, however, no one individual is justified before God or saved. This truth does not diminish the forgiveness that was applied to mankind in Christ's resurrection; justification has come to all (Rom. 5:18), even though it is not personally received apart from the Word of forgiveness and the faith it creates.

Many false and inaccurate statements have been made about proponents of objective justification. It is said that "This is universalism," regarding this thesis: "Christ is the Savior of all. This means that the whole world of sinners has been redeemed, forgiven, and reconciled to

---

[1]Gregory Jackson, *Luther versus the Pietists*, 44.

[2]Gregory Jackson, *Luther versus the Pietists*, 27.

[3]Joshua Sullivan, "Objective Justification: Part One," *Ask the Pastor* (2015; http://www.youtube.com/watch?v=O-y90Eqwx-Y).

God in Him."[4] Strangely enough, the opposite has also been said to be the case: "general justification as taught by [those who hold to objective justification] has as its logical sequence strong synergistic elements," so that it is illogically said that man cooperates in his salvation.[5] An ELDoNA pastor insinuates that objective justification "caused people to say: 'justified saints in hell'," as if it were an inevitable conclusion.[6] This talking past one another and putting words in others' mouths is not of Christ. Of course, all talk of saints in hell is fruitless and speculative—tell such a person who misuses Scripture with their logic to go ahead and preach to the damned. There is obviously a substantial disagreement, but much of the talk is baseless and politicizing attacks, not based on a concern for scriptural teaching. The truth of the matter is that each side is operating with a completely different framework and way of understanding the diverse statements of Scripture.

There is a failure to really study and consider the matter carefully, and to communicate with the objective to promote understanding. A particular discussion on this topic revealed that "there have been misunderstandings, unclear thinking, and poor communication because of overstatements, lifting of phrases and snippets of doctrinal expression out of context, and sometimes even pressing of casual expressions to ultimate conclusions not intended by the speakers."[7] Over time, this creates mass confusion regarding this critical teaching of Scripture, which is not only unhealthy, but in fact contrary to God's Word: "But avoid foolish controversies, genealogies, dissensions, and quarrels about the law, for they are unprofitable and worthless" (Tit. 3:9).

This controversy has long been seen as a political forum to attack the heart of opponents' Lutheran identity. The same exact arguments appear over a century ago. In an 1889 article, the author "quotes the Law against the Gospel proclaimed in objective justification, as well as quotes passages that speak of justification by faith, as if by doing so the possibility of a justification before faith is ruled out."[8] In a different generation: "Reconciliation and personal justification are

---

[4] Gregory Jackson, *Luther versus the Pietists*, 124.

[5] Vernon Harley, "Synergism—Its Logical Association with General Justification."

[6] Joshua Sullivan, "Objective Justification: Part One."

[7] Robert Preus, "Objective Justification."

[8] Henry August Allwardt (1840–1910). Rick Curia, *History of Objective or Universal Justification*, 53.

lumped together as one, so that nothing is left of the justification of the individual through faith," so that it is "annihilated."[9]

Unable to grasp both scriptural aspects at the same time, logic overcomes the truth, so that "what is said about subjective justification is supposed to rule out what Missouri says about objective justification."[10] Objective justification "surely wipes out 'justification by faith alone,' of which the Scriptures speak page after page."[11] This is one of the main problems with the modern denial of objective justification: it assumes a contradiction between two scriptural data points where there is none. Today ELDoNA confesses: "One cannot correct a supposed insufficiency by contradiction."[12] The deniers claim that objective justification "suggests that St. Paul repeatedly wavered and contradicted himself as he moved between justification by faith and justification without faith."[13] Scripture confesses both strands undiminished; thus scriptural teaching must uphold both, so that one does not impede or trample the other.

There is truly nothing new under the sun. Some have more recently supported this old, unreasoned attack: "to be justified" no longer means "to be declared righteous," "but merely to appropriate something subjectively," which includes "even Judas and all unbelievers."[14] But the scriptural teaching says that "all have a share in justification," not that all are saved apart from Christ and faith in Him.[15] The underlying assumption of all modern deniers of objective justification is that there are not different facets to justification.

One reason this error is so pernicious is that it sounds very Lutheran. It only wants to stick to the most traditional language of several hundred years ago, taking refuge in the words of past orthodox Lutherans. As was pointed out in 1867, though, traditional words can be twisted and made to say something other than what they originally meant: "One

---

[9]R.C.H. Lenski, quoted in: Rick Curia, *History of Objective or Universal Justification*, 60.

[10]Rick Curia, *History of Objective or Universal Justification*, 63.

[11]Lenski, *Commentary on Romans* (1936), quoted in: Rick Curia, *History of Objective or Universal Justification*, 87.

[12]ELDoNA, "Theses on the Article of Justification," 4.

[13]Editorial note by Gregory Jackson in: Vernon Harley, "Synergism—Its Logical Association with General Justification."

[14]Gottfried Fritschel, quoted in: Rick Curia, *History of Objective or Universal Justification*, 29.

[15]George Stoeckhardt, "General Justification," 141.

is not faithful to the truth because he uses correct expressions, when he means them to say something else."[16] "Justification by faith" is a mere slogan, but it is presented as if these three words can express the fullness of the mystery of how we receive God in Christ. It is deceptive and satanic to rely on words formulated by one's fathers, and yet use them to communicate something they did not say. But the issue is much more than what man has said: the matter can only be concluded with Scripture's authority.

> Passages from Scripture or the Book of Concord that speak of justification in subjective, personal terms cannot be used to refute objective justification. In the same way, passages that speak of justification in general, objective, or universal terms cannot be used to refute subjective justification. The reinforcement of one does not undercut the other. Passages that teach objective justification are used to teach objective justification, while passages that teach subjective justification are used to teach subjective justification.[17]

It is the same principle that God's consuming wrath at sin does not undermine His grace found in Christ.

The logical implications that are clear in the minds of the opponents of objective justification are, in actuality, denied in practice by those who uphold that justification is complete in Christ. Universalism is categorically false—not all are saved. Faith is necessary to receive the benefits of justification in Christ, and the actual communication of the Gospel must deliver these gifts. Actual statements must document one's position, not what an enemy thinks he must logically believe.

Also, it is unfair and dishonest to conflate all understandings and uses of objective justification terminology, both historical and modern. It becomes hard to pin down exactly what is being rejected. To a large extent the terminology bears the brunt of the attack, rather than the confessed doctrine. The basic assumption that the duality of justification is on its face impossible and absurd will not let the deniers of objective justification see the most basic distinctions that are carefully laid out: not the terms themselves, but how they are used is the pressing matter. To deny and forbid words, especially when one is "justification," is petty and untheological.

---

[16]Ulrik Vilhelm Koren (1826–1910), quoted in: Rick Curia, *History of Objective or Universal Justification*, 22.

[17]Jon Buchholz, "Jesus Canceled Your Debt!," 11.

Justification is a verdict, a declaration of righteousness, or, as 2 Cor. 5:19 defines it, the non-imputation of sins. It is a revealed, divine teaching. It is not a human fact to manipulate. From God's side, the verdict pronounced on Christ allows the Gospel to be a true pardon and bestowal of forgiveness. The fact that people reject this verdict and application, ultimately receiving no conferral, appropriation, imputation, or benefit, does not mean the pardon made by the Father over mankind in Christ is void and null. This is true even to a human court:

> United States v. Wilson, 32 U.S. 150 (1833), was a trial in the United States in which the defendant, George Wilson, was convicted of robbing the US Mail in Pennsylvania. Due to his friends' influence, Wilson was pardoned by Andrew Jackson. Wilson, however, refused the pardon. The Supreme Court was thus asked to rule on the case.
>
> The decision was that if the prisoner does not accept the pardon, it is not in effect: "A pardon is a deed, to the validity of which delivery is essential, and delivery is not complete without acceptance. It may then be rejected by the person to whom it is tendered; and if it is rejected, we have discovered no power in this court to force it upon him." Therefore, Wilson was not released from prison early.[18]

In the end, Wilson refused President Jackson's forgiveness from the death penalty, but that rejection did not make the President's pardon less than truthful, valid, and effective.

The defenders of objective justification accuse the deniers of faulty logic: "The [ACLC] critique points out [ELDoNA's] logical fallacies thesis by thesis. In general, the conclusions of the theses are built on three fallacies: Straw Man, Equivocation, and Exclusion."[19] ELDoNA responded by accusing the ACLC of "using equivocal wordings that make an attempt at meaningful discussion of this topic frustrating," because they do not consistently define the term objective justification. This is labeled as "patently misleading."[20] Again, this is nothing new: "Would it not be much better that our opponents, if they see fit to give us instructions in regard to what is church-language and what is not, would make the matter a subject of earnest study first, so that they

---

[18]"United States v. Wilson," Wikipedia, The Free Encyclopedia (http://en.wikipedia.org/w/index.php?title=United_States_v._Wilson&oldid=869356490).

[19]Abstract, ACLC, "Critique of ELDoNA."

[20]Eric Stefanski, "Theses on the Article of Justification: A Refutation of the ACLC's Critique: Part One."

may know something certain about this thing they say or whereof they affirm?"[21] Under the guise of simplicity and making justification clear is the refusal to deal with new errors: "The Lutherans from the age of orthodoxy understood the simplicity of the article of justification."[22] It will not do to gloss over what does not fit into simple, historical formulas of speech. Salvation has never been simple or without difficulty to man's reason. Christ's doctrine, especially this most precious article of justification—which is the center of Christian hope—deserves defense at all cost. Party politics and human words dare not obstruct what Christ actually gave in Scripture. As a part of, and basis for, justification, "There is no Lutheran theology apart from Objective Justification."[23]

---

[21]F.A. Schmidt, quoted in: Rick Curia, *History of Objective or Universal Justification*, 28.

[22]Paul Rydecki, "The Forensic Appeal to the Throne of Grace in the Theology of the Lutheran Age of Orthodoxy: A Reflection on Atonement and its Relationship to Justification," Colloquium of the Evangelical Lutheran Diocese of North America, Malone, Texas (April 30, 2013; http://eldona.org/ELDoNA/Papers_files/ForensicAppeal_Rydecki_Final.pdf), 1.

[23]Martin Diers, "Objective Justification," 19.

Chapter 8

The Resurrection Effect

In the Scriptures, Christ's resurrection is not simply a historical occurrence dealing only with Christ Himself, and neither is it an add-on, an extra, to the Christian confession. But the modern Protestant "idea of atonement does not have much room for resurrection which can go almost unmentioned because it is not required."[1] In Scripture, though, Christ's rising from the dead does not have less to do with our salvation than His death. The two are intimately connected, according to Scripture, as without Christ's rising there is no forgiveness. "And if Christ has not been raised, then our preaching is in vain and your faith is in vain" (1 Cor. 15:14). So Christ's death alone does not signal completion of mankind's salvation: "if you confess with your mouth that Jesus is Lord and believe in your heart that God raised him from the dead, you will be saved" (Rom. 10:9).

If just Christ's death, the price of His payment for sin, is spoken of, we have a part of the Gospel, not the whole thing. Without the acceptance of His sacrifice, the actual discharging of our debt, God is not reconciled. The Father's acceptance of Christ's payment, signaling the propitiation of His wrath, is the reconciliation which says that sins are not imputed to sinners in Christ. This new relationship of God to sinful humanity is the truth safeguarded by objective justification. The

---

[1]Charles Pinnock, quoted in: Lee Tankersley, "Raised for Our Justification: The Resurrection and Penal Substitution," *The Southern Baptist Journal of Theology* 18:4 (Winter 2014; http://equip.sbts.edu/publications/journals/journal-of-theology/raised-for-our-justification-the-resurrection-and-penal-substitution).

acceptance of Christ as our substitute and the fruit of the atonement are the central issues in this modern denial of objective justification.

Justification is clearly and prominently tied to faith in Scripture, but if it is only related to faith, so that man's faith makes the Gospel true and a new relationship with God possible, everything centers on the sinner, rather than the Savior of all. In this schema faith makes Christ's death acceptable to the Father and replaces the resurrection: Christ's death is still the price, in theory, but God Himself is unpropitiated and unreconciled—His wrath has *not* been addressed by Christ.

Scripture expressly says that justification is wider than faith in one sense. It ties justification directly to Christ's historical resurrection from the dead (Rom. 4:25). The question then arises: What changes the relationship between God the Father and humanity as a whole? It cannot be faith, since not all believe. So, to the deniers of objective justification, God is still wrathful, and forgiveness only exists for believers. This forgiveness happens at the point of faith, so that mankind is under God's wrath, and only His wrath. Accordingly, every individual sinner, outside of faith, is under divine wrath, but, in Christ, Scripture speaks of another connection to humanity that makes the Gospel truly good news. "He is the propitiation for our sins, and not for ours only but also for the sins of the whole world" (1 Jn. 2:2). The result of that propitiation is that "now through Christ the human race which offended God was reconciled to an irate and alienated God, and thus by this very action God was pacified."[2] The death of Christ cannot be considered apart from His resurrection: "And you, who were dead in your trespasses and the uncircumcision of your flesh, God made alive together with him, having forgiven us all our trespasses, by canceling the record of debt that stood against us with its legal demands. This he set aside, nailing it to the cross" (Col. 2:13–14). The resurrection of Christ is the complement to Christ's death—without it, Christ's sacrifice, if narrowly considered, is of no worth to man.

Very few deniers of objective justification have been willing to tackle 2 Cor. 5:19, because it is difficult to ignore the teaching of objective justification without denying these plain words of Scripture: "that is, in Christ God was reconciling the world to himself, not counting

---

[2]Balthasar Meisner (1667), quoted in: Robert Preus, "Justification as Taught by Post-Reformation Lutheran Theologians," 8.

their trespasses against them, and entrusting to us the message of reconciliation." One attempt at interpreting this critical passage makes reconciliation a present action in response to the Gospel: "Therefore it hadn't yet occurred that God had reconciled the world to himself, for now the ambassadors first come with the exhortation, 'Be reconciled to God!'. . . . [2 Cor. 5:19] describes justification as a fruit and consequence of reconciliation: *so that we might become the righteousness which avails before God.*"[3] Various interpretations have been attempted, but no sustained and convincing explanation of 2 Cor. 5:19 has been offered by the Lutheran deniers of objective justification.

Another denier speculates that 2 Cor. 5:19 says "nothing about a past event." Instead of confessing a past universal act in the body of Christ, this pastor claims it means merely that "Jesus was in Palestine forgiving and healing."[4] The word "world" used in 2 Cor. 5:19 becomes a very small subset of humanity in this denial of Scripture: "world," in this instance, actually refers to those Jesus encountered and forgave in His personal ministry. This severs the atonement and Christ's resurrection— His salvific ministry and acts—from reconciliation. Why this undoing of Scripture, which teaches a universal justification? It is due to the false assumption that "Justification is always a present tense thing."[5] Though that is often how Scripture talks, we see that it is also connected with, and originates from, the resurrection of Christ.

Those who deny objective justification must make the reconciliation of 2 Cor. 5:19 a momentary activity, not part and parcel of the redemptive work of Christ. Reconciliation, then, has nothing to do with God, but only "a change in men (their conversion). In the immediate context of verse 19 Paul says that God reconciled . . . 'us' (Paul and his assistants in the ministry) to Himself. That is, God brought them to faith through Christ."[6] In another attempt at evading the plain sense, God's world reconciling is said to be an example of Paul's teaching:

> Verse 19 and those following give a sample of the Gospel message brought by Paul and his assistants. They proclaim that God in connection with Christ (whose redemption paved

---

[3] John Klindworth (1833–1907), quoted in: Rick Curia, *History of Objective or Universal Justification*, 62.

[4] Joshua Sullivan, "Objective Justification: Part Three."

[5] Joshua Sullivan, "Objective Justification: Part Four."

[6] Maier, "A Summary Exposition of Justification," 26.

the way for God's saving activity . . .) was engaged in reconciling (was engaged in this ever since the time of Christ's public ministry and the completion of his redeeming work on Calvary, and during the years subsequent to his resurrection up to the time Paul writes) the world to Himself (that is, those people in the world in whom God through the Holy Spirit and in connection with Christ worked effectively to accomplish their regeneration), not imputing their trespasses to them (that is, forgiving their sins as they were brought to faith).[7]

This interpretation confines God's reconciling to Christ's preaching ministry, so His atoning work has no immediate effect or relevance. In v19–20, however, all preaching activity is shown to be dependent on what Christ actually did and the new relationship between God and the world. "Therefore, we are ambassadors for Christ, God making his appeal through us. We implore you on behalf of Christ, be reconciled to God. For our sake he made him to be sin who knew no sin, so that in him we might become the righteousness of God" (2 Cor. 5:20–21). God, the reconciled party, is the one making the appeal through the Gospel to unreconciled man. Unbelievers do not appeal to and reconcile God as the promise is communicated. Sins can be forgiven because they are already forgiven in Christ.

This attempt to explain away the text of 2 Cor. 5:19 makes a critical mistake, reversing the direction of reconciliation:

> The present-tense participles in this verse in no way indicate a one-time act of "having forgiven" or "having justified" all people that supposedly took place at the cross. *God uses means to reconcile people to Himself.* Through the ministry of the Word, He brings people to Christ the Reconciler and does not impute sins to believers in Christ (clearly expressed in Rom. 4:5–8). This verse [19] from 2 Corinthians does not teach that the world has already been justified, and was never used by any of the Lutheran Reformers to teach such a thing.[8]

The action has been reversed: what God does presently in the Word—reconciling people to Himself—is substituted for what Christ already did: "in Christ God was reconciling the world to himself." While it is true that people are brought back to God by the "word of reconciliation,"

---

[7] Maier, "A Summary Exposition of Justification," 28.
[8] Emphasis added. Letter from Rydecki to President Jon Buchholz.

God is reconciled by Christ's action, on behalf of the world, in this particular verse. But this is skipped over, because God, for the denier of objective justification, is not reconciled until faith comes.

There seems to be no real reconciliation of God to mankind, in theory or practice, for modern deniers of objective justification. Accordingly, man is solely the problem, and God's wrath does not necessitate a new relation to man as a whole. The root of this error shows a different conception of God, of His wrath, and the need for its propitiation. So, by default, the resurrection of Christ as the vindication and reconciliation of mankind is passed over. It becomes a mere historical fact, with no import for the Gospel. As a denier of objective justification boldly stated: "The Resurrection of Christ was only one absolution among others, not THE absolution of the world."[9]

Without mankind's justification, the debt payment is theoretically existing, but Christ is effectively dead before faith comes to the individual. The payment is not yet accepted and the debt is not discharged. "Justification by faith alone" should not be twisted to mean that no aspect of justification is in existence before faith comes. If justification depends on faith totally, it has no connection to Christ, "who was delivered up for our trespasses and raised for our justification" (Rom. 4:25). It is claimed that objective justification "point[s] hearts to a declaration not recorded in Scripture, but that they assert (based on questionable exegesis that would be foreign to the early Lutherans) was made in the heart of God on Good Friday (or Easter)."[10]

That Christ's resurrection is our justification is clearly scriptural. "Great indeed, we confess, is the mystery of godliness: He was manifested in the flesh, vindicated by the Spirit, seen by angels, proclaimed among the nations, believed on in the world, taken up in glory" (1 Tim. 3:16). The vindication of Christ was a public act of acquittal—a declaration of forgiveness and the acceptance of all that Christ had done. The question is: Who was Christ's resurrection for? "Christ did not need acquittal for Himself, for no one can accuse Him of a single sin. Who therefore was it that was justified in Him? Who was declared pure and innocent in Him?

---

[9] Thesis of Larry Darby, quoted in: Kurt Marquart, "Objective Justification," *Marquart's Works*, 6:87.

[10] Eric Stefanski, "Theses on the Article of Justification: A Refutation of the ACLC's Critique: Part One."

We were, we humans. It was the whole world."[11] Christ's vindication is the public recognition that His death and payment for all sin has been transacted and applied, so that God is reconciled and pleased with sinners in the person of Jesus.

Man's reason cannot harmonize two simultaneous verdicts: one in Adam and one in Christ. This requires dulling the meaning of 2 Cor. 5:19, because of "The absurdity of a pre-existent declaration given to all men that then must be taken away if [there is] unbelief."[12] If objective justification is true, the law has no validity and universalism must result, it is argued, but this rational approach minimizes the variety with which Scripture and the Confessions speak. For example, in its article on justification, the *Apology to the Augsburg Confession* "identifies justification with reconciliation (114, 161, 181), with regeneration (72, 78, 117, 181, 292), with remission of sins (72, 75, 114), with forensic righteousness (72, 305), and with vivification (250)."[13] While there are nuances, of course, there is also great biblical overlap in the usage of the term "justification."

How does the assumption of an unreconciled God, who can only be wrathful, affect the Gospel message? It must, even if ever so subtly, become law. "Christ's resurrection means that all who hope in him, all who trust in him, all who look to him for forgiveness of their sins are absolved before God's courtroom in heaven. The empty tomb means the justification of all who believe in the risen One."[14] Absolution is removed from the Gospel message itself, and placed far away from man when there is no reconciliation because of Christ. Although one may speak this way, since believers do possess Christ's justification, it is not the complete picture, since believing is not the critical component to justification. Christ "was delivered up for our trespasses and raised for our justification" (Rom. 4:25). The Gospel gives forgiveness because Christ is absolved—and us through Him—in His resurrection.

The Gospel, without any objective aspect, is robbed of forgiveness, as this quote demonstrates: "This is not a 'pronouncement' that all men

---

[11]Walther, Easter sermon, quoted in: Robert Preus, "Objective Justification."

[12]Joshua Sullivan, "Objective Justification: Part 4."

[13]Martim Warth, "Justification through Faith in Article Four of the Apology," 119.

[14]Paul Rydecki, Easter Sermon (April 8, 2012; http://www.intrepidlutherans.com/2012/04/remember-jesus-christ-risen-from-dead.html).

are righteous. This is the righteousness of Christ that would serve to justify the whole world of sinners, if the whole world of sinners would believe in Christ."[15] But Paul does not condition the extent or power of justification which came as a result of Christ. A possible future justification, provided man meets God's criteria of faith, is not a biblical justification at all. It is the equivalent of saying that because Adam sinned, all might be condemned who meet the condition of being a "sinner" in the future. But Rom. 5 speaks of Adam as the origin and cause of our sinful nature, not that we have the option of becoming sinners if we take certain steps. Sin is universal and has come to all through Adam. The verdict of righteousness in Christ parallels the reign of sin over all mankind. The difference is that we are not in Christ by natural birth, so that without faith His righteousness is not yet possessed.

On the other hand, we are born into sin so that we are actually sinful. But our sinful birth did not cause Adam to sin and humanity to be cursed—it is the other way around. Neither does our believing make righteousness available in the Gospel or God forgiving. No, quite the opposite, we believe that God is forgiving because He is reconciled in Christ and actually forgives in the Gospel. Although the parallel in Rom. 5 must not be pressed too far in regards to *how* the verdicts are received, the *realities* of sin and forgiveness—the justification of the world in Christ—are not dependent on man's reception of them.

> In Romans 4:25 the apostle joins the payment of punishment rendered for us through the death of Christ, as cause, with the justification, i.e. the remission of sins acquired in Christ's resurrection, as effect. Paul is not dealing with renewal here—something he discusses at length in chapter 6—but he is discussing the imputation of righteousness, as the whole sequence of the chapter shows.[16]

Scripture—God's very mouth—intertwines the objective, completed aspect of justification into this context of speaking about believers, who are justified by faith. "That is why it depends on faith, in order that the promise may rest on grace" (Rom. 4:16). "That is why his faith was 'counted to him as righteousness.' But the words 'it was counted

---

[15] Paul Rydecki, "The Forensic Appeal to the Throne of Grace," 35.

[16] Quenstedt, quoted in: Robert Preus, "Justification as Taught by Post-Reformation Lutheran Theologians," 8.

to him' were not written for his sake alone, but for ours also. It will be counted to us who believe in him who raised from the dead Jesus our Lord, who was delivered up for our trespasses and raised for our justification" (Rom. 4:22–25).

A key aspect to untangling this debate is noting *when* the reconciliation of God is completed: in Christ, at His resurrection, or in faith, when the "condition" of the Gospel is met. Some who deny objective justification say that God "reconciled these enemies and made them friendly toward Himself ('reconcile,' according to Webster: 'to make friendly again or win over to a friendly attitude') in the miracle of conversion—this gracious action of God made possible by, based upon, mediated by the death of his Son,"[17] but then there would only be God's wrath in the Word. Faith within the believer, not Christ in His body, would be what actually effects forgiveness in the Father.

The Lord's death is inextricably linked to His rising. If the actual act of resurrection has no theological significance, Christ's work waits for its completion: "Christ was raised so that He *might* justify sinners."[18] This makes the Gospel only a roadmap to potential forgiveness. In Christ, therefore, nothing actually brought righteousness upon man, and neither does the Gospel actually offer anything: "they transform the forgiveness of sins . . . into the potential of a later forgiveness of sins."[19] This is a most dangerous side effect of denying the completion of Christ's work: "All these benefits ['adoption, the remission of sins, eternal life, salvation, regeneration, and the giving of the Holy Spirit'] belong to Christ. He has obtained them all on behalf of all men, and wishes to distribute them to all men through the Gospel, and in that sense they are universal."[20] He either actually distributes forgiveness in the Gospel (but not the fruits denoting renewal, which are only spoken of in connection to faith) or He does not. A "wish" or motivation to forgive implies that faith has to move God to actually grant forgiveness. It means no one is actually given anything in the Gospel itself.

Christ's payment or procurement alone, as one step in the process of justification, is an incomplete salvation. God's wish and willingness

---

[17] Maier, "A Summary Exposition of Justification," 25.

[18] Emphasis added. Joshua Sullivan, "Objective Justification: Part Two."

[19] George Stoeckhardt, "General Justification," 142.

[20] Paul Rydecki, "Francis Pieper's Misuse of Romans 4:25," 19.

to forgive—even His love for mankind—is not something that deals with His wrath and anger at sin. God is either reconciled, by Christ, or unreconciled. For the denier of objective justification, "Paul is teaching nothing in 2 Corinthians 5:19 but the very same thing that Jesus taught as recorded in John 3:16–18. God loved the world. God gave His Son as a sacrifice to [potentially] reconcile the world to Himself. All who believe in the Son are reconciled with God. Those who don't believe in Him remain in condemnation."[21] An unreconciled god does not allow a real, forgiving Gospel. Outside the Gospel absolution in Christ, everything is cursed, and God is a consuming fire (Heb. 12:29): "The patriarchs knew the promise of the Christ, that for his sake God intended to forgive sins."[22] If sinners are not given Christ's righteousness to actually rely on, the so-called "Gospel" is then a demand for something from man, not forgiveness from God. The desire of God to forgive, or the death and resurrection of Christ as merely the first step toward absolution, is a message of wrath, pure and simple.

What happened in Christ is for the benefit of all. It is un-Christian to limit His work in any facet. According to one ELDoNA pastor, "[Johann] Gerhard [1582–1637] does, indeed, say that Christ was absolved of the sins of the whole world; but he does *not* say that the whole world now stands absolved."[23] This quote by a denier of objective justification claims that what happened to Christ in *His death* was substitutionary for mankind, but not what took place in *His resurrection*—so the world is not absolved, only Christ Himself.[24] This makes it seem as if our Lord needed absolution for His own person, not that what happened to Him was done in the stead and on behalf of those for whom He died. In

---

[21]Paul Rydecki, blog comment on "Luther's Translation of 2 Corinthians 5:19" (Feb. 1, 2013; http://www.intrepidlutherans.com/2013/02/luthers-translation-of-2-corinthians-519.html).

[22]Maier, "A Summary Exposition of Justification," 7.

[23]Eric Stefanski, "Theses on the Article of Justification: A Refutation of the ACLC's Critique: Part Two,"

[24]Jonathan Edwards refutes this conception, even with his Calvinism: Christ "was not acquitted as a private person, but as our head, and believers are acquitted in his acquittance; nor was he accepted to a reward for his obedience as a private person, but as our head, and we are accepted to a reward in his acceptance. The Scripture teaches us, that when Christ was raised from the dead, he was justified." *Sermons and Discourses, 1734–1738,* in *The Works of Jonathan Edwards,* ed. M. X. Lesser (New Haven, CT: Yale University Press, 2001), 19:191.

explaining away Gerhard's words, the assumption is that justification is solely the product of faith. This reinterpretation of Gerhard's clear confession that "Christ was absolved of the sins of the whole world" is easy for a modern denier of objective justification, because faith supposedly wipes out every thought of justification's basis: "It is often the cause of great misunderstanding to cite one or two sentences from a Church Father as proof of a doctrine, especially when those sentences are only a minuscule representation of a much larger discussion."[25] Clearly, for Gerhard, as for the Holy Spirit, the resurrection causes our salvation and makes personal justification possible: Christ's absolution is credited to mankind. Gerhard says that Christ's resurrection was on behalf of mankind, so that "the resurrection of Christ may be both the cause and the pledge and the complement of our justification."[26]

Walther is ridiculed for connecting absolution to Easter so poignantly: "the Easter absolution nonsense of Walther," they call it.[27] But "the idea of the great Easter absolution of Christ, which constitutes our righteousness, comes from Luther's description of the resurrection."[28] Luther dared to teach that because of Christ's completed work all are justified—that is, offered this righteousness—so all are righteous in Christ.

> Isaiah here [53:11] uses the word "many" for the word "all," after the manner of Paul in Rom. 5:15. The thought there is: One has sinned (Adam), One is righteous (Christ), and many are made righteous. There is no difference between "many" and "all." The righteousness of Christ, the only-begotten Son of God, our Lord and Savior, is so great that it could justify innumerable worlds. "He shall justify many," says he, that is to say, all. It should, therefore, be understood of all, because He offers his righteousness to all, and all who believe in Christ obtain it.[29]

Luther did not limit the righteousness of Christ, the extent of justification.

> For as we see in the first picture on Good Friday, how our sin, our curse and death are put upon Christ, so we see

---

[25]Paul Rydecki, "Francis Pieper's Misuse of Romans 4:25," 16.

[26]Quoted in: Paul Rydecki, "Francis Pieper's Misuse of Romans 4:25," 19.

[27]Gregory Jackson, *Luther versus the Pietists*, 40.

[28]Magnus Sørensen, "The Justification of Christ," 26.

[29]Martin Luther, "Isaiah 53," quoted in: *Luther Says: An Anthology,* ed. Ewald M. Plass (Saint Louis: Concordia Publishing House, 1959), 608.

on Easter Day another picture, where there is no sin, no
curse, no displeasure, no death but only life, grace, bliss
and righteousness on Him. With such a picture we should
establish our hearts. Then it is shown and given to us that
we should receive Him in no other way than as if God has
raised us today with Christ.[30]

For Luther every instance of the Gospel is valid, because justification
of life came to all in Christ's resurrection.

From this command [of Christ in Jn. 20:21–23] we also
have the power to comfort the sorrowful consciences and to
absolve from sin, and we know that, wherever we exercise
this office, not we but Christ himself is doing it. Therefore
every Christian, in this case as well as when he hears the
Word preached in the pulpit, should hear the same, not as
the word of man, but as the Word of God himself; then
he can indeed be sure and need not doubt a moment that
he has the forgiveness of sins, for Christ has established
through his resurrection that whenever a called servant of
the Church, or someone else in the time of need, absolves
his neighbor who is distressed and desires comfort, it shall
count as much as if Christ had done it himself, because it
was done at his command and in his name.[31]

What Christ accomplished reconciled God to mankind, and this justification is given in the Gospel which absolves. Christ's forgiveness in the
Gospel is what faith rests on. We believe that when Christ was raised,
we were raised with Him, cleansed of sin and fully absolved.

Objective justification has been helpfully defined as "a summary
declaration of the effect of world redemption."[32] Christ was raised
not only to make a statement about Himself and for His own benefit,
but "also to free others from sin and destruction."[33] "When ELDoNA
denies that Christ needed to be absolved from our sins and turns his
resurrection into a mere vindication of him, they are wrong."[34] ELDoNA
teaches:

Christ's "justification" is, rather, the vindication of One who
both is innocent by nature and by conduct and who has

---

[30] Quoted in: Tom Hardt, "Justification and Easter," 54.

[31] Emphasis added. *Complete Sermons of Martin Luther*, 1.2:397.

[32] George Schweikert, "Notes on Objective Justification," *Confessional Lutheran*
VI (1945), quoted in: Rick Curia, *History of Objective or Universal Justification*, 3.

[33] Abraham Calov, "Selections from Abraham Calov's *Biblia Illustrata*," 21.

[34] Magnus Sørensen, "The Justification of Christ," 27.

paid for the sins of all others. The fact that the Christ was
made sin for us (2 Corinthians 5:21) and bore our sins as
His own (Psalm 69:5) does not require Him to be absolved,
since, again, He was not forgiven for our sins (forgiveness
requiring someone else to pay the debt). Instead, He Himself
paid the debt.[35]

The payment was made, but, in this thinking, it is not accepted, and
God is not said to be satisfied. This false teaching seems to indicate
that if Christ had remained dead, and not been raised, the Gospel
would be unchanged. Perhaps this is their gospel, one that has as much
power as the true Gospel would if Christ had not been resurrected:
"And if Christ is not risen, then our preaching is empty and your faith
is also empty. Yes, and we are found false witnesses of God, because
we have testified of God that He raised up Christ, whom He did not
raise up" (1 Cor. 15:14–15). The scriptural parallel is broken: He died
because of our sins, but was only raised for His own person, not for all
sinners. But the great teaching of the resurrection as the reception of
Christ's payment is essential to faith and forgiveness, according to God.
Without a resurrection, Christ's death—the payment of His life—counts
for nothing.

It is stubbornly claimed that "Luther, Chemnitz and Melanchthon
did not see any world justification in 2 Cor. 5:19. On the contrary,
they saw Paul highlighting the ministry of the Word and teaching
justification only through faith in Christ."[36] This astute answer, from a
non-Lutheran, shows how the nature of the Gospel itself declares that
God is reconciled by Christ already:

> It is further pertinaciously [stubbornly] argued, that the New
> Testament language contains no such expression as God's
> reconciliation to man. This, as has been already noticed,
> is not necessary; and the entire gospel is an indubitable
> proof of this. It is nowhere said, in any proclamation of
> the gospel among Jew or Gentile, that they must reconcile
> God to themselves; for it is God who is always represented,
> and in the most natural way, as reconciling men to Himself
> by Jesus Christ (2 Cor. 5:18–21). But how was this done?
> Not by granting absolute remission of sins, not by a simple
> cancelling of the trespasses committed by us; but solely by
> putting Christ, as a representative, in their place to do what

---

[35] ELDoNA, "Theses on the Article of Justification," 7.

[36] Paul Rydecki, blog comment on "Luther's Translation of 2 Corinthians 5:19."

they could not have done, and by inviting men upon the ground of that atonement, to be reconciled to Himself in a mediator. The whole transaction shows two things—the love of God's heart, and the rectitude of His government. All who refuse the atonement are, from the necessity of the case, left standing on their own footing as sinners, and out of divine favour; whereas all who receive the atonement are reconciled.[37]

Stated another way, we must be able to answer the question: Who is the Gospel for? The Gospel is absolution. It is not just talk about a theoretical forgiveness, but the specific power that takes away sins before God. This is what the Gospel both declares and bestows. Despite the fact that many are condemned, despising Christ's absolution, this does not nullify the fact that "the justification of life has come upon all men."[38] This objectivity of the Gospel is not a technical point, but the basis for every powerful communication of Christ.

Those avoiding talk of objective justification will have trouble with this question: Is forgiveness for the whole world actually available, so that the Gospel can be boldly preached as a divine, absolving Word? This summary, in question form, meant to show the poor logic of objective justification, is basically correct:

God has forgiven all people, but if you don't believe, then you're forgiven but not forgiven, even though all people are forgiven, and you stand both righteous and condemned before God at the same time. ????? . . .

Jesus saved all people, but not all people are saved. ?????

All people were justified before they were born, but stand condemned already at the time of their birth. ?????

God has changed the status of all people to "righteous," but still counts unbelievers among the "unrighteous." ?????[39]

The verdicts, judgments, and declarations of God's condemnation and salvation are universally in effect. While not clear-cut to sinners, this is exactly what allows both the law and the Gospel to be preached undiluted in content and undiminished in power. Sin must be exposed,

---

[37]George Smeaton, *The Doctrine of the Atonement as Taught by the Apostles; or the Sayings of the Apostles Exegetically Expounded* (Edinburgh: T & T Clark, 1870; http://archive.org/details/doctrineofatonem00smea), 132.

[38]F.A. Schmidt, quoted in: Rick Curia, *History of Objective or Universal Justification*, 27.

[39]Letter from Rydecki to President Jon Buchholz.

condemned, and forgiven.

"For if Christ was not raised from the dead, there would not be faith, . . . and Christ would not be able to apply righteousness to us."[40] "The justification of the world in Christ is something that actually happened to Jesus, when He was brought forth from the grave."[41] The basis, power, and impetus for our subjective justification is Christ's objective, redeeming work, not man and his faith. But the other side contends: "Christ's resurrection is not the whole of our justification."[42] It is not the whole picture of *personal* justification, but it is a logical error to say that because Christ's resurrection is not everything concerning the matter of justification, it is not the essential foundation. Our justification is complete in Christ, but in regards to its reception it is not complete— the Gospel is still going out to justify sinners. Objective and subjective justification are one and the same: "Thus through faith the general justification becomes a special justification."[43] Only in this duality may we be faithful to justification by faith alone and the completed fact that Christ was "raised for our justification" (Rom. 4:25).

---

[40] Abraham Calov, "Selections from Abraham Calov's *Biblia Illustrata*," 23–24.

[41] David Jay Webber, "Our Righteousness before God," 47.

[42] Paul Rydecki, "Francis Pieper's Misuse of Romans 4:25," 20.

[43] George Stoeckhardt, "General Justification," 143.

Chapter 9

The All-Encompassing Role of Faith

The question is not whether faith is a work or a gift, but the timing of God's acceptance and the propitiation of His wrath. Christ's payment was completed at His death, but when is it accepted, and when are sinners declared free from God's wrath? This determines the results, benefits, and consequences of the atonement (Christ's death). Forgiveness was won, both sides agree, but how is it applied and when is it an earthly reality? This is a central question of our day that early Lutherans did not have to focus on—the issue for them was personal appropriation (which is by faith alone). We do not expect people unacquainted with a modern and novel error to speak directly to it, so looking only to past men's words and old slogans is not a way out of this controversy, as the deniers would wish. The three words "justification by faith" cannot express the fullness of the Gospel. Neither can the two words "objective justification," so it needs to be investigated on the basis of God's revealed Word.

Without an objective basis to forgiveness and an aspect that depends only on the finished work of Christ, the Gospel, no matter how eloquently spoken, is an illusion, a figment, a mere possibility—not a present reality distributed in words. This is an essential component to forgiveness, even though it was not always explicitly stated in the past. "Faith in Christ does not justify and save because, as an excellent work of man, it acquires a bountiful merit before God, and as a satisfaction for sin reconciles Him unto man."[1] Faith receives what Christ accomplished and the Father gives because He is reconciled. The act of believing does not satisfy God in a way similar to Christ's death. Neither does it complete the transaction of salvation in Christ.

This is an agreeable statement to some who deny objective justification: "The doctrine of Justification is understood by us to be that an individual is subjectively (i.e. personally) declared righteous before God when he believes in objective righteousness that is provided in Christ for the whole world."[2] "Provided" can be understood to mean that some of the arrangements have been made, but righteousness is not yet completed or in effect. But the "in Christ" should indicate that it is complete, since this righteousness or forgiveness is given by Him and actually received by faith. What is rejected by some in this orthodox-sounding language is that forgiveness is currently applicable—it has been partially prepared, they admit, but does exist for all in Christ. In truth, however, it has been made available, ready-made, for the whole world in Christ. Christ did not fail in His aim to be the Savior of all and defeat sin.

We are not talking about the earning of righteousness, but its fulfillment, so that forgiveness is presented in the Gospel itself. If the price has been acquired, but not accepted, so that God indicated His satisfaction, there is no actual forgiveness as a result. The process is incomplete. Here we are talking of the results of the acquisition and merit of Christ—what happened and what was declared as a result of Christ's resurrection. Does the merit (the price) lay unclaimed and ineffective until faith completes the transaction, winning justification for itself? The issue is not the reception of forgiveness, but the basis of justification.

This purely subjective presentation of justification does not allow for any blessings to exist before faith: "When faith is present to lay hold on Christ's merits, the sinner's justification occurs; the forgiveness of sins is granted; God's condemning wrath against the sinner ceases; sinners have reconciliation with God, life, the other blessings of present salvation,

---

[1]Theses accepted at the first convention of the Synodical Conference (1872), quoted in: Rick Curia, *History of Objective or Universal Justification*, 37.

[2]ACLC, "Critique of ELDoNA," 3; Eric Stefanski, "Theses on the Article of Justification: A Refutation of the ACLC's Critique: Part One."

and the eternal heavenly inheritance."[3] If faith precedes forgiveness, it *makes* it happen in some way. Faith itself becomes a propitiatory sacrifice, made to placate an angry god. This teaching of a personal-only forgiveness leaves man with only a "Gospel" of wrath.

Is righteousness (forgiveness which must be applied) created in or by faith? There is no way around stating what is objective about forgiveness. This conclusion is correct: "The efficacy of the Word is the point of contention."[4] As important as the means of grace are, if they are disconnected from God's reconciliation in Christ, they become magic words. In effect, they replace Christ's historical atonement. In this denial of objective justification we end up with the conclusion that every communication of the Gospel is sacrificial and propitiatory, denying "the offering of the body of Jesus Christ once for all" (Heb. 10:10). It was not Christ's death alone that ended all sacrifice to God, but His ascension in resurrection glory: "But when Christ had offered for all time a single sacrifice for sins, he sat down at the right hand of God" (Heb. 10:12). The means of grace deliver a perfect and completed justification—they do not perfect the reconciliation of God to man. "For by a single offering he has perfected for all time those who are being sanctified" (Heb. 10:14).

The finished nature of justification allows the Gospel to deliver what already exists: the forgiveness of sins. If it is not a present reality, faith activates the atonement in this scheme, making Christ's work effective—meaning that, of itself, Christ's death was good, but did not actually change anything with the Father. That happens in time—not in Christ—if faith is made to be a simple conditional cause of salvation. "God was in Christ, reconciling the world" is redefined to mean that "after God was in Christ, God is reconciled in (believing) man." But as the Confessions state, faith is receptive, relying solely upon Christ: "in justification before God faith relies neither upon contrition nor upon love or other virtues, but upon Christ alone, and in Him upon His complete obedience by which He has fulfilled the Law for us, which [obedience] is imputed to believers for righteousness" (*Formula of Concord* [FC] SD 3:30). Relying on "Christ alone" is the same as being justified by "faith alone," which means it is all from Christ and His Work.

---

[3] Maier, "A Summary Exposition of Justification," 9.

[4] Gregory Jackson, *Luther versus the Pietists*, 23.

In essence, without objective justification, Christ rises for forgiveness in each believer—not by the Spirit on the third day. This makes each person the missing ingredient of forgiveness. We may not limit the effect of Christ's justification because we do not see all men trusting it and benefiting from it. All are justified in Christ, but not all are saved.

> The whole notion of "special faith," [Ap 12:45, 59], which is "conceived of the Gospel or absolution," [AC 12] presupposes a real, objective treasure of forgiveness [Ap 4:103–105] brought into existence for all men by the work of Christ, and really and truly offered, distributed, and communicated to them in the means of grace, to be appropriated and received by faith alone.[5]

The disagreement is not over faith, or its importance, but what it relies on and what lies behind it. So both sides must be emphasized: "On the one hand forgiveness is the result of faith, and thus comes after faith, and on the other hand it is the object of faith and therefore goes before faith."[6] But Scripture is clear that without Christ's resurrection, which led to justification for all mankind, all faith is in vain (1 Cor. 15:14).

Christ was sacrificed for forgiveness once—not daily in acts of faith. It is not the shedding of faith's blood that cleanses. Jesus not only earned, acquired, and made forgiveness a possibility, He brought it forth for all men. Faith can be made a work more valuable than everything Christ did in the flesh—indeed, this is the understanding of many Protestants.

---

[5]Kurt E. Marquart, "No 'Hoax' Maier and Objective Justification," *Marquart's Works,* 10 vols., ed. Herman J. Otten (New Haven, MO: Lutheran News, 2014–15), 6:68.

[6]Kurt E. Marquart, "The Reformation Roots of Objective Justification," *A Lively Legacy: Essays in Honor of Robert Preus,* eds. Kurt E. Marquart, John R. Stephenson, and Bjarne W. Teigen (Fort Wayne: Concordia Theological Seminary Press, 1985; http://www.ctsfw.net/media/pdfs/MarquartReformationRootsofObjectiveJustification.pdf), 117.

Chapter 10

In Christ and Outside of Christ

Careful wording of the objective aspect of justification, following the scriptural precedent, is always qualified by where it is found: in Christ. In the 19th century, this was virtually always the case. For example, notice how the phrase "in Christ" prevents any universalist connotations: " . . . all men are truly redeemed from sin, death, devil and hell, in Christ as the second Adam, and God is truly reconciled with them all."[1] This is also made evident by a theologian who later organized the "Anti-Missouri Brotherhood" and opposed Walther on predestination: "by the resurrection of Christ He has been absolved from the sins of the whole world, and that *in Him* as Mediator and representative surely *the whole world had been justified,* because He was justified from the sins of the whole world."[2] This simply follows the pattern of Scripture: "*in Christ* God was reconciling the world to himself, not counting their trespasses against them" (2 Cor. 5:19). This forgiveness is not found in the world or man's sinful nature, so no individual is forgiven apart from Christ. No person is in Christ without the hearing of the Gospel, repentance, and faith. Our verdict of righteousness is in Christ, the one who was vindicated for us and our sin.

The forgiveness of all people in Christ was not indiscriminately

---

[1] Thesis 4, Walther, *Justification—Objective and Subjective,* 8.

[2] F. A. Schmidt, quoted in: Rick Curia, *History of Objective or Universal Justification,* 21.

applied to individuals until more recently. Originally, it seems that "the terms [of objective and subjective justification] were made known to Walther through an article in a theological paper in Germany, printed in 1867," which said that "Objective justification affects 'humanity as a collective, in which the particular individuals are not separate entities but are inherent parts of a totality.'"[3] The words "world" and "mankind" indicate everyone, in general, but not any one particular person. So the phrase, "the world was absolved in Christ," does not conflict with all individuals being condemned sinners in Adam—that is, the flesh. This qualification of "in Christ" is highly significant in speaking of the world's pardon. "General justification was . . . a public forensic declaration happening in Christ as our representative."[4] Objective justification, the effect of Christ's work, cannot be separated from Christ and what He did to redeem the world.

Christ, the one made to be our sin, was absolved, but He was a substitute in our place, and, therefore, we were absolved by proxy. The Father declared us guilt-free in Christ, who was our representative. This physical absolution happened publicly to Christ, in His resurrection, not outside of Christ.

> By raising Jesus to life, God declared the world's sin paid for, he declared Christ to be absolved (justified) of the world's sin that had been charged to him, and he declared the world to be justified in Christ as the world's substitute. In Christ as its stand-in, the world has been justified before God through and because of its resurrected substitute, Christ Jesus.[5]

The use of words like "world," "mankind," and "humanity" in regards to the general justification that has already happened in Christ preserves the duality of justification. From Christ's side, sins are forgiven, absolved, and taken away. Forgiveness is complete and accomplished in Christ, but we are not born naturally into Christ, so we must be born anew to God by water and the Word. "Truly, truly, I say to you, unless one is born again he cannot see the kingdom of God" (Jn. 3:3).

Objective justification, or general justification, as it was more commonly termed in the 19th century, is a worldwide reconciliation. From

---

[3] Tom Hardt, "Justification and Easter," 65.
[4] Magnus Sørensen, "The Justification of Christ," 12.
[5] Jon Buchholz, "Jesus Canceled Your Debt!," 6.

God's side, He is fully reconciled—all sins are truly forgiven in Christ, "Thus reconciliation is parallel to justification."[6] But the reception of this forgiveness has to do with individuals—real subjects who are born into Adam, as indicated by the term "subjective justification." Objective justification and subjective justification may not be defined in whatever way one wishes. The fine distinction between them is critical—one side of reconciliation will be lopped off if it is not maintained. Outside of Christ, God is still angry at sin and damns the unbeliever because he is still in Adam, under the curse of the law. It is this unresolved tension regarding God's view of mankind, one in and one outside of Christ, that has led to the modern denial of objective justification. In the pattern of the twin verdicts of law and Gospel, the distinction between the world's objective justification in Christ and one's individual justification "corresponds exactly to the biblical distinction between God's own completed reconciliation of the world to Himself in Christ (II Cor. 5:19) and our reconciliation to Him by faith (v. 20)."[7] If one side is eliminated, we have lost the truth of Scripture—the reality of both the law as God's wrath and the Gospel as absolution. The Lutheran teaching of the keys—the binding and loosing of sins—tells us both are real and effective—neither cancels the other out.

Objective justification describes God's relation to the world, as a whole. This real justification in Christ is a result of Christ's finished work, but it does not mean the sins of individuals need not be forgiven or addressed with the law.

> The apparently contradictory statements of Scripture, that the world is absolved, and that guilt rests upon unbelievers as long as they do not repent, must be solved in this [way]: We must distinguish [between the] two ways in which God views mankind. When He views the world in Christ, He looks upon it with infinite love, but when He beholds it out of Christ, He can no otherwise than behold it with fiery indignation.[8]

---

[6] *katallásso*, *Theological Dictionary of the New Testament: Abridged in One Volume*, eds. Gerhard Kittel and Gerhard Friedrich, trans. Geoffrey W. Bromiley (Grand Rapids: William B. Eerdmans, 1967), 41.

[7] Kurt Marquart, "Objective Justification," *Marquart's Works*, 6:71.

[8] Discussion of theses accepted at the first convention of the Synodical Conference (1872), quoted in: Rick Curia, *History of Objective or Universal Justification*, 37.

Or as another translation puts it: "When God regards the world in Christ, His Son, He looks at it with the most fervent love; but when He regards the world outside of Christ, then He cannot look at it otherwise than with burning wrath."[9] God's justification of the world does not mean that sin is magically wiped away from every sinner, so that all possess eternal life. This objective justification is in Christ, not outside of Him.

According to Rom. 5:18, the twin verdicts are universal, but without opposing one another: "Likewise then, as by the offense of one, the fault came on all men to condemnation, so by the justifying of one, the benefit abounded toward all men to the justification of life" (1599 Geneva Bible [GNV]). In Christ all are justified, but in Adam all are condemned. Christ's justification

> is the great absolution which took place in the resurrection of Christ. For as the Father, for our sake, condemned His dear Son as the greatest of all sinners by causing Him to suffer the punishment of the transgressors, even so did He publicly absolve Him from the sins of the world when He raised Him up from the dead. And us in Him.[10]

Rom. 5:18 "implies that Adam and Jesus are unique; none other affects the world as these two."[11]

That the world was justified "in Christ" is critical, since it preserves the condemnation of the law as a reality. Unbelievers "place themselves outside of that relation of God to sinners which has been established and has validity only in Christ and which is declared to sinful men only in the Gospel."[12] Our unbelief does not diminish the result of Christ's justification, but to deny the objective aspect of justification is to hold that God is not reconciled. "The wrathful God after all cannot offer forgiveness, but only that God who, as He has revealed it in the Gospel, loves all in Christ, because they have been acquired through Him."[13]

One of the main motivations in denying objective justification is to not contradict God's wrath and the reality of sin. Its deniers cannot hold the condemnation "in Adam" and the justification "in Christ" together

---

[9]Walther, *Justification—Objective and Subjective*, 10.

[10]Preuss, *Justification of the Sinner before God*, 8.

[11]Lee Tankersley, "Raised for Our Justification."

[12]George Stoeckhardt, "General Justification," 143.

[13]Walther, *Justification—Objective and Subjective*, 13.

at the same time. As a consequence, God's reconciliation to man is done away with as an objective event—man is not justified from God's vantage point. Objective justification requires and declares that God was objectively reconciled as a result of Christ's redemptive action: "For God was in Christ, and reconciled the world to himself" (2 Cor. 5:19; GNV). To repudiate objective justification is to say that God's reconciliation is not necessary before man's reconciliation to God in faith. The reconciliation of God to man, if it exists at all, is thus only a present activity which occurs as a result of faith:

> God required no reconciling by Christ in the sense that the work of Jesus was necessary, so that God could generate his love toward sinful unregenerate mankind: "God so loved the world, that He gave his only begotten Son" (Jn. 3:16). The situation rather is this: the Father's eternally existing love conceived, and in Christ executed, the plan of redemption and salvation for the sinful human race, so that He could graciously extend salvation to believers. Unregenerate sinners, who are simultaneously the objects of God's wrath and his love, desperately need Spirit-wrought reconciliation (the "being made thoroughly other" in conversion), so that, with justifying faith present in their hearts, God may remove his condemning wrath from them and give them the blessings of salvation. God in his grace does grant both reconciliation and justification, and He does so simultaneously—the one gift is a change worked within sinners, as He turns them from unbelief to faith in the Lord; the other, a pronouncement made upon them, as He declares them righteous through the faith implanted in them.[14]

So Christ, in His own body and work, did not change God's relationship to man—God is still wrathful—but, evidently to the denier of objective justification, He does not need to be reconciled. Love is then the possibility, or the impulse, to bring about forgiveness. It does not, however, mean that there is anything besides God's anger at sinners. The relationship painted, from God's point of view, is then one-sided in the law, without the objective aspect of justification. Without an objective reconciliation, there is only wrath, therefore, there can only be a message of wrath for man. God's love is not a replacement for what His love caused Him to do, accomplish, and bring about in the sacrifice of His Son: the forgiveness of sins. This supposed "Gospel" does not reveal that God's anger has been stilled in Christ, nor inform man of

---

[14]Maier, "A Summary Exposition of Justification," 25–26.

God's objective reconciliation.

It is the divine dialectic of law and Gospel that makes this full topic of justification unsettling to those who mock objective justification. They want it to be simple, plain, and clear, without any difficulties.

> While the Law certainly declares all men to be guilty and deserving of death, the Gospel does not declare all men to be righteous. The Gospel declares that the righteousness of Christ stands in for all who trust in Him and is reckoned or imputed to believers, so that if the whole world were to believe in Christ, then the whole world would be declared righteous.[15]

The "Gospel," note, does not actually do anything here. A gospel that only declares that certain persons may be righteous is not the true Gospel. This "Gospel" cannot address man's condemned state, since there is no prior justification in Christ. In this heresy, faith, not the Gospel of a reconciled God, is what personal justification depends on. That is because, in this view, faith is what allows God to be gracious and forgiving, not Christ's historical work. There is no objective forgiveness, here, because not all come to faith. Not Christ, but faith, satisfies God's wrath against the believer. This approach does simplify things quite a bit, but it leaves mankind with only a wrathful God—one unwilling to actually forgive all sins for the sake of Christ. There is no possible contradiction between law and Gospel because there is only law, at least until faith makes a non-wrathful God possible.

Scripture speaks differently than man would have God speak. The word "justification," in English, when used universally, is a true verdict. It is said to be dependent solely on Christ, and is therefore in effect. The same word for justification, δικαίωσις, in Rom. 4:25 and Rom. 5:18 "means the act of justification by the divine acquittal . . . and [is used] with reference to the whole existence of man before God."[16] Christ is the second Adam, and this righteous pardon came "just as sin came into the world through one man, and death through sin, and so death spread to all men because all sinned" (Rom. 5:12). The reality of a gracious God is now present, even more than the reality of sin, "For if many died through one man's trespass, much more have the grace of God and the free gift by the grace of that one man Jesus Christ abounded for many"

---

[15]Paul Rydecki, blog comment on "Luther's Translation of 2 Corinthians 5:19."

[16]"δικαίωσις," *Theological Dictionary of the New Testament*, 2:223.

(Rom. 5:15). This justification is "much more" than the verdict in Adam. This truth allows sinners to use the full comfort given in the Gospel against the grave condemnation of sin the law displays, as Luther did: "If Christ is the price of my redemption, if He put Himself under a curse in order to justify me and bless me, I am not put off at all by passages of Scripture, even if you were to produce six hundred passages in support of the righteousness of works and against the righteousness of faith."[17]

The use of the law against the basis of the Gospel is endemic among deniers of objective justification. Scripture confesses that Christ "is risen again for our justification" (Rom. 4:25; GNV). This objective securing of justification is received by man in faith, but depends solely on Christ. Because He is alive, justified in His rising for us, we may be justified in time, but this clear passage is corrupted by those who challenge objective justification, because it makes the Gospel of a reconciled God possible before faith. The interpretation, therefore, of Rom. 4:25 is "so that we *might* be justified, *through faith*," because that "is consistent with the immediate context of chapter four in which it is found."[18] This "faith" overrides anything prior to faith and its very own foundation: Christ's justifying resurrection.

It is the failure to uphold the twin verdicts of law and Gospel that causes such mischief. However, this is precisely the point that is eluded or denied when objective justification is discarded. The deniers claim that the position of the LCMS is, according to its 1932 "Brief Statement," that "God has already declared the whole world to be righteous."[19] This is a deliberately dishonest citation. The phrase "in Christ" is purposely and maliciously left off, to make it look un-Christian. The "Brief Statement" actually says: "Scripture teaches that God has already declared the whole world to be righteous in Christ, Rom. 5:19; 2 Cor. 5:18–21; Rom. 4:25."[20] Leaving out the "in Christ" is an enormous error in a precise formulation, and it completely changes its meaning.

This key error is also made in the official ELDoNA theses: "In the

---

[17]"Lectures on Galatians" (1535), LW 26:295.

[18]Emphasis added. Maier, "A Summary Exposition of Justification," 23.

[19]Eric Stefanski, "Theses on the Article of Justification: A Refutation of the ACLC's Critique: Part 9."

[20]*Brief Statement of the Doctrinal Position of the Missouri Synod* (St. Louis: CPH, 1932; http://www.lcms.org/Document.fdoc?src=lcm&id=958), 6.

resurrection, it is said, God actually absolved the world."[21] Although the "in Christ," may, at times, be assumed from the context and overall doctrinal picture, this sort of cherry-picking makes theological dialogue impossible. Without the "in Christ," objective justification would be open to charges of universalism, but the "in Christ" qualifies it, because not all individuals are in Christ. Ironically, this exact same method is used by the most liberal Lutherans to defend homosexual activity and transgenderism: "There is neither Jew nor Greek, there is neither slave nor free, there is no male and female, for you are all one in Christ Jesus" (Gal. 3:28). Since we are not fully in Christ, but must live in this world, we do distinguish between genders and their divinely created roles. To assert that what is true "in Christ" is physically true in the world, among those still fully in Adam, is un-Christian.

Just as the reality of justification in Christ—that God is fully reconciled—does not deprecate the power of the law in condemning sin, so the world's justification in Christ does not subvert the personal justification of the individual by faith. In fact, one cannot be had without the other. "It is impossible to separate once-for-all justification at the cross and personal justification in faith."[22] It is the truth that there is no anger for man at his sin—but only forgiveness and justification—in Christ. This allows the Gospel to deliver the goods of forgiveness, which actually justify those in Adam. So the Gospel itself justifies, because justification is complete and finished as of Christ's resurrection.[23] This is what comes to us in time: "For although the work is accomplished and the forgiveness of sins acquired on the cross, yet it cannot come to us in any other way than through the Word" (*Large Catechism* 5:31).

---

[21] ELDoNA, "Theses on the Article of Justification," 1–2.

[22] "δικαιόω," *Theological Dictionary of the New Testament*, 2:216.

[23] The issue of disputing the timing of justification—or how Old Testament saints were justified before the resurrection of Christ—is to apply human restrictions to God. We are not talking about the event, but its effect on man, which is solely based on "the Lamb slain from the foundation of the world" (Rev. 13:8). Abraham was counted righteous by faith in Christ. He did not have to wait for his offspring (Jesus) to be born for this forgiveness (righteousness)—it came in the promise and he received it.

Chapter 11

Removing Christ: Deforming Objective Justification

The careful wording of 19th century theologians has in many instances been lost in succeeding years, completely deforming the doctrine of objective justification, even as it goes by the same name. This makes the debate quite tricky to untangle adequately. A change in the way some define and speak about objective justification has been evident since the early 20th century. It is mainly, but not exclusively, associated with the Wisconsin Synod—especially certain professors at the former Wauwatosa Seminary near Milwaukee.

While early WELS pastors were trained by the Missouri Synod and spoke like Walther, this new seminary inculcated "an originality of thought," calling on those who wish to practice theology "to throw off the shackles of preconceived notions and to do original work regardless of whether one is working with Scripture or not."[1] The movement associated with these Wauwatosa professors, sometimes called the "Wauwatosa

---

[1]Mark Braun, "The Wauwatosa Gospel" in *Lord Jesus Christ, Will You Not Stay: Essays in Honor of Ronald Feuerhahn on the Occasion of his Sixty-Fifth Birthday,* ed. J. Bart Day, et. al. (Houston: The Feuerhahn Festschrift Committee, 2002; reformatted: http://www.dropbox.com/s/iptsqfo27ayn2kx/Braun_Wauwautoa_Gospel.pdf, 32.

theology" or "gospel,"[2] occurred in the first third of the twentieth century, until the seminary moved in 1929. These WELS professors—who had been taught by Walther at Concordia, St. Louis—showed appreciation for Missouri's doctrine, but also reacted slightly against Walther.

As ELDoNA correctly indicates: "Note, that among LCMS theologians [objective justification] is not generally stated as 'all men,' but as 'Mankind' or 'the world,' so that the 'class' is absolved, but no persons in particular. Among the WELS theologians, this distinction doesn't seem to be maintained."[3] This has major implications for how the doctrine of objective justification is understood.

One of the earliest shifts in this doctrine is noticeable in the WELS professor John Schaller:

> God on His part made the reconciliation of the world a reality, is reconciled to the whole world, has made peace with it. . . . He then of necessity forgave the sins to this same world, justified it. What is more, He did not justify the concept world, nor the world as a whole of which some small parts could possibly be missing, without invalidating the statement. On the contrary, He consciously declared righteous every individual who belonged to the world or will belong to the world to the end of days, every individual sinful person. But this is *universal justification.*[4]

While the first part of this statement is praiseworthy, the logical application of this teaching, that mankind is justified in Christ, to individuals outside of Christ marks a dramatic shift in logic. Although it was done to emphasize the Gospel, this new approach changes the nature of objective justification and cannot be supported biblically.

When Scripture deals with individuals, it speaks in terms of faith and unbelief. Justification, outside of any one person, deals with the whole of sinful humanity. This justification happened to Christ and is found in Christ—not in the natural children of Adam. To speak of objective justification in terms of particular persons changes the whole nature of objective justification. "Apart from Christ there exists no forgiveness to

---

[2]Paul Hensel wrote a book in 1928 entitled: *The Wauwatosa Gospel: Which Is It?* (Marshfield, Wisconsin).

[3]ELDoNA, "Theses on the Article of Justification," 2.

[4](1910), quoted in: Rick Curia, *History of Objective or Universal Justification,* 68–69.

be distributed. We could say, 'God has forgiven the entire world,' but the statement remains incomplete (and could even be abused in favor of universalism) until we clarify, 'God has forgiven the entire world in Christ.'"[5] This statement, made by a WELS leader, is a reaction against the Wauwatosa move of applying objective justification to unbelieving individuals.

The step of applying the verdict of objective justification to individuals, instead of to humanity as class, lived on in the WELS: " . . . God declares the unbeliever just. The fact that the unbeliever by rejecting God's verdict deprives himself eternally of the joy and comfort that this message gives does not make the declaration of God untrue."[6] Even the man who followed Walther as the most influential theologian in Missouri, Franz Pieper, in his still significant dogmatics work, seems to come across this way: "the resurrection of Christ from the dead is the actual absolution pronounced upon all sinners." But a more literal translation renders it: "the resurrection of Christ from the dead is an actual absolution of the whole sinful world."[7] Carelessness has overtaken this doctrine in the 20th century, making it seem more dubious.

Why the move to apply an objective verdict to individuals? It was done in the name of Gospel, but the law is implicitly dulled in the process. This prevents the full verdict of condemnation on one still in Adam, indicating that even "without faith one is not under the wrath of God and eternally lost."[8] While this seems like the logical implication of objective justification, this critical move completely alters the entire doctrine of justification: "If it is true that God has forgiven the sins of the world then it is also true that he forgave the sin of Judas. When Jesus called Judas 'friend' in the garden, he was in effect treating him as a forgiven sinner."[9] What was said earlier to condition the objective aspect—the qualifier "in Christ"—was consciously or unconsciously dropped.

---

[5] Jon Buchholz, "Jesus Canceled Your Debt!," 22.

[6] Siegbert Becker, "Objective Justification," 12.

[7] The German reads: "der ganzen Sünderwelt sei." "Justification: Objective vs Subjective—Walther in America; Count Erbach (Pieper's *Dogmatik*)" (Dec. 2, 2016; http://backtoluther.blogspot.com/2016/12/justification-objective-vs-subjective.html).

[8] CTCR, "Theses on Justification," 17.

[9] Siegbert Becker, "Objective Justification," 15.

Another Wauwatosa professor, J.P. Meyer (1873–1964), became the center of a controversy long after his death. The 1979 Kokomo affair is traced to statements of Meyer dating to 1955 and one statement of obscure LCMS origin, compiled by two couples belonging to a WELS church in Kokomo, Indiana. These four "theses" on objective justification were assembled by laymen who denied the teaching, so they are not true theses. Meyer's statements, taken from his republished commentary, were not put in the best light, since they were culled by two couples completely unsympathetic to what he meant to express. These "Kokomo theses" became a watershed for many in WELS. This was unfortunate because they neither are precise, nor technically correct. Some (mostly in WELS and those in fellowship with her) have put them in the best possible light and defended them, but most LCMS theologians, who also hold to objective justification, have rejected these theses in totality.

Remember that they were drawn for a negative purpose, to ridicule objective justification, not to clarify it. They read:

> 1. Objectively speaking, without any reference to an individual sinner's attitude toward Christ's sacrifice, purely on the basis of God's verdict, every sinner, whether he knows it or not, whether he believes it or not, has received the status of a saint.

> 2. After Christ's intervention and through Christ's intervention, God regards all sinners as guilt-free saints.

> 3. When God reconciled the world to Himself through Christ, He individually pronounced forgiveness on each individual sinner whether that sinner ever comes to faith or not.

> 4. At the time of the resurrection of Christ, God looked down in hell and declared Judas, the people destroyed in the flood, and all the ungodly, innocent, not guilty, and forgiven of all sin and gave unto them the status of saints.

In a letter containing these statements, sent to all WELS congregations, the charge of universalism was made: "We could not with a clear conscience support those statements since they teach universalism and are contrary to the clear teachings of the Holy Scriptures and the Lutheran Confessions."[10] The compilers of these "theses" clearly tried to

---

[10] Quoted in: David J. Beckman, "Universal and Objective Justification with Special Emphasis on a Recent Controversy," District Pastor-Teacher Conference of the South Atlantic District (Jan. 27, 1983; http://essays.wls.wels.net/bitstream/handle/123456789/373/BeckmanUniversal.pdf), 1.

make a caricature of the doctrine and put it in the worst light possible. These four statements unfortunately became a litmus test for objective justification in WELS, and were defended in principle by some, but not all in WELS universally defended them; one leader has called them "reprehensibly imprecise" and "unacceptable." He also said that this mixture of universal teaching and subjective terms "should be roundly rejected by the WELS as an incongruous mishmash."[11]

On the other hand, a WELS pastor stated that "Those who read Meyer in context should have no problem with what he says here. . . . "[12] One of the leading WELS theologians of that era said: "The third statement is a basically good summary of our position, although on the part of those who believe that we do not consider faith to be important enough, it probably needs the wider content of our stress on *sola fide* [faith alone]."[13] This acceptance of the logic of the Kokomo statements, by the same professor, marks a stark contrast from 19th century formulations: "If it is true that God has forgiven the sins of the world then it is also true that He forgave the sins of Judas."[14] This is not how Scripture speaks—it is a pure fabrication of sinful reason.

The "in Christ" language consistently used in the 19th century is now routinely left out. Logic is carried to an unbiblical conclusion: if it happened to the world, then it happened to each individual. "This [declaration] applies to the whole world, to every individual sinner."[15] It might seem like a small point, but this leap transgresses the scriptural boundary laid down by God, disconnecting forgiveness from Christ. Like the denial of objective justification, it is a misuse of human logic, despite the best intentions of preserving the character of the Gospel.[16]

As it turns out, the opposite of an error is almost always an error in itself. Following the biblical pattern, faith is always connected to an

---

[11] Jon Buchholz, "Jesus Canceled Your Debt!," 40.

[12] Rick Curia, *History of Objective or Universal Justification*, 103.

[13] Siegbert Becker, "Objective Justification," 14.

[14] Siegbert Becker, "Objective Justification," 15.

[15] This is the basis for the third Kokomo statement. J.P. Meyer, quoted in: Rick Curia, *History of Objective or Universal Justification*, 103.

[16] Of course, in hell there is no Gospel preaching or means of grace. "The doctrine of objective justification does not imply that there is no hell, that God's threats throughout Scripture to punish sins are empty, or that all unbelievers will not be condemned to eternal death." Robert Preus, "Objective Justification."

individual's justification. "Saint" and other such individual words only apply to those on earth with faith.

The Kokomo caricature caused some to accept what has long been an exaggeration of objective justification. In 1867 the president of the Augustana Synod erroneously summarized objective justification, in an attempt to paint it as absurd: "The whole world—even Judas—has been justified and has received the forgiveness of sin. . . . (even Judas) has become a child of God and an heir of heaven."[17] This same language, however, is frequently found today in works promoting objective justification. This is the logic of universalism, even if that conclusion is ultimately rejected: If Christ is the Savior of all, then all are individually saved.

Right after the Kokomo affair, the issue of objective justification rocked the LCMS, due to the teaching of a Fort Wayne seminary professor who was a candidate for synodical president. Eventually, after some public skirmishes,[18] the professor affirmed objective justification. The controversy resulted in a thorough set of theses for the LCMS on justification in 1983, which led to a renewed appreciation for the scriptural teaching of objective justification. The theses also explicitly reject the Kokomo-style exaggerations and carelessness:

It is contrary to Scripture and the pure Gospel to teach:

That Christ's work of atonement is of such a nature that even those who do not believe receive justification to life and salvation;

That without faith one is not under the wrath of God and eternally lost;

That it is proper to speak of saints in hell or to

---

[17]T. N. Hasselquist, quoted in: Rick Curia, *History of Objective or Universal Justification*, 2.

[18]Walther A. Maier II articulated perhaps the most clear, honest, and forthright denial of objective justification in the modern age, which was subsequently retracted: "I regret that some publicly quoted statements of mine from a technical paper 'prepared for faculty discussion purposes only' have given a wrong impression about my doctrine of justification as a whole. I, therefore, withdraw that paper from discussion. Doctrinally, I stand with our Synod's historic position." Robert Preus, "Objective Justification." His 1982 paper questioning objective justification is used in this work merely as an example to illustrate the logic of how objective justification can be questioned, not to assess or impugn his views. Evidently, it was sent to LCMS congregations by concerned laymen. Maier, "A Summary Exposition of Justification," 1–2.

use similar expressions in describing justification;

> That there can be anonymous Christians, that
> is, those who have not had access to the means
> of grace but nevertheless believe without true
> repentance and faith in Christ, of whom they
> have never heard and about whom they know
> nothing.[19]

The charge has been made recently that the LCMS holds to a version of objective justification that includes particular individuals: "Those who claim that the LCMS version of objective justification does not apply to individuals, but only to mankind as a whole, cannot so easily discount [Franz] Pieper's citation of Meyer."[20] This is not the WELS J.P. Meyer of Kokomo infamy, but a German theologian older than Walther: Heinrich August Wilhelm Meyer (1800–1873). While this man had no evident connection to the Missouri Synod, a particular footnote citing him in Pieper's dogmatics has been used twice, 35 years apart, to argue against Missouri's teaching of objective justification.[21] Heinrich Meyer's comment on 2 Cor. 5:18 reads, in the English translation of Pieper:

> Mankind was on account of its uncanceled sins under God's
> holy wrath, ἐχθροὶ Θεοῦ [enemies of God], Rom. 5:10, *Deo
> invisi*, the object of God's hatred; but with the cancellation
> of their sins, effected by the death of Christ, God's wrath
> came to an end. The reconciliation of all mankind took place
> objectively through the death of Christ.[22]

Despite the fact that a citation in a footnote is not a full and unqualified endorsement, Meyer himself is more careful. The context is clearly speaking about the result of Christ's work, not that there is no wrath at all for unbelievers. In fact, an English translation of Meyer has been in existence since 1877,[23] in which he says that, in 2 Cor. 5:19, the word "world" "applies to *the whole human race*, not . . . merely to those predestinated. The reconciliation of all men took place objectively

---

[19] CTCR, "Theses on Justification," 17.

[20] Paul Rydecki, "Francis Pieper's Misuse of Romans 4:25," 4.

[21] Maier, "A Summary Exposition of Justification," 15.

[22] Paul Rydecki, "Francis Pieper's Misuse of Romans 4:25," 4; F. Pieper, *Christian Dogmatics*, 2:348; Heinrich August Wilhelm Meyer, *Critical and Exegetical Handbook to the Epistles to the Corinthians* (New York: Funk and Wagnalls, 1884; http://play.google.com/books/reader?id=FkRDAAAAYAAJ), 535.

[23] Heinrich Meyer, *Hand-book to the Epistles to the Corinthians.*

through Christ's death, although the subjective appropriation of it is conditioned by the faith of the individual."[24] Again, he comments:

> The former ["He does not reckon to them their sins"] is the altered judicial relation, into which God has entered and in which He stands to the sins of men; the latter ["has deposited in us the word of reconciliation"] is the measure adopted by God, by means of which the former is made known to men. From both it is evident that God in Christ reconciled the world with Himself; otherwise He would neither have left the sins of men without imputation, nor have imparted to the apostolic teachers the word of reconciliation that they might preach it.[25]

It is clear that Rydecki irrationally attacks the translation of a citation, without checking its original context.

The first comment of Meyer, taken in concert with the second, speaks of mankind as a unit. It confesses the finished result of Christ's Work—reconciliation—from the side of God. In Christ, there is no wrath for man, only justification. This judgment comes to us in the Gospel. What Meyer's quotation does prove, since the passage in question appears in the original German as early as the year 1840,[26] is that Rydecki's, and his synod's (ELDoNA), claim that this teaching is a Synodical Conference or "Waltherian" invention is false. Although the LCMS was not founded until 1847, Rydecki speaks of the "Waltherian doctrine of objective justification:" "it should be clear to all that Pieper, following Walther, took a single phrase from Scripture out of context, and a single sentence from those Fathers out of context, and constructed a modified doctrine of justification out of it. . . . "[27] He accuses Walther of "imagining an already-existing justification of the world as necessary for justification by faith to occur, and then reading his modified views back into the Lutheran Fathers, and back into the Scriptures themselves."[28] This inability to honestly debate the issue is the fruit of trying to fit others' words into a very limited rational framework, which denies the full scope and import of God's Word.

---

[24]Heinrich Meyer, *Hand-book to the Epistles to the Corinthians*, 537.

[25]Heinrich Meyer, *Hand-book to the Epistles to the Corinthians*, 537.

[26]Heinrich August Wilhelm Meyer, *Kritisch exegetisches Handbuch über den zweiten Brief an die Korinther* (Göttingen: Vandenhoeck und Ruprecht, 1840; http://play.google.com/books/reader?id=t_AUAAAAYAAJ), 115.

[27]Paul Rydecki, "Francis Pieper's Misuse of Romans 4:25," 1, 28.

[28]Paul Rydecki, "Francis Pieper's Misuse of Romans 4:25," 7.

The spurning of objective justification is rooted in the failure to consider the dual verdicts of law and Gospel as simultaneous and universal, seeing them, instead, as mutually exclusive. "Now, if the wrath of God against men has been stilled by Christ's atoning sacrifice, what is it, pray tell, that still damns unbelieving sinners? What shall be done with Paul's statement about the day of wrath in Romans 2:5–12?"[29] Scripture, however, teaches both without contradiction.

There is still a real difference among those who use and defend the term objective justification. While the LCMS, in its written confessions and among its esteemed theologians, follows the more careful pattern of Walther and Pieper, the Wauwatosa influence is still felt in WELS. One of its public statements on justification, advertised on its website as "What we Believe," reads:

> The Bible and Lutherans teach that God judged all sinners righteous in his sight when Jesus Christ died on the cross for us. God declared everyone free from the guilt and punishment owed for our sins. The sinner receives this free gift of forgiveness, not by doing good deeds, but only by faith. A person is justified when he or she believes in Christ and his redemptive work. It is a gift from God.[30]

This is not how Lutherans spoke before the 20th century. "Everyone" could be understood collectively, but this justification is not qualified by "in Christ." It leaves much to be desired.

This change in language easily leads to a re-definition of the Gospel: "[This] is the message of all Christian mission work: *'God has pardoned you.'* Do not reject your pardon, but accept it by believing in the Lord Jesus Christ."[31] This assumes an effective individual pardon prior to the hearing of the Gospel, but is one to trust an unknown, non-verbal justification, or the one that exists in Christ and is delivered in the Gospel? The Gospel can become a simple reminder, rather than a true impartation of forgiveness, if objective justification becomes the whole of justification. If unbelief is the only sin, then one can rule out using the law to condemn actual sins. God's wrath is not just directed at unbelief, but over all sin of those in Adam. There is no actual forgiveness in the

---

[29] Maier, "A Summary Exposition of Justification," 15.

[30] http://wels.net/about-wels/what-we-believe/.

[31] *100 Questions and Answers for Lutherans of the Synodical Conference* (1954), quoted in: Rick Curia, *History of Objective or Universal Justification*, 137.

Gospel if there is only past forgiveness. That leaves very little to trust in, since everything is put into the past, having nothing to do with the sinner today.

The justification of the world in Christ is not simply a fact to take for granted, but a real, present, and vital forgiveness bestowed on the individual. There is an objective aspect of justification, but also a subjective aspect, dealing with its actual reception in time. God's wrath is not a figment, a mere scarecrow, so that we need not fear the law. "The Law of God is His serious will. His wrath is not a mere illusion on the part of guilty man, but a divine reality—the inevitable reaction of His holiness and righteousness against sin and the sinner."[32] The scriptural duality of forgiveness in Christ and wrath in Adam must be maintained to preserve the strength of God's truth.

Only in the abuse of applying objective justification to unbelieving individuals, is this true: "objective justification always wants to put the justification of the sinner back in the past."[33] There is no justification to trust in for the sinner, as an individual, before the Gospel comes. Justification is a present action for each man, a real bestowal of forgiveness, which the Word distributes. Both excesses are due to human reason stretching the scriptural facts too far. The sinner is not the cause of forgiveness, nor is justification all in past, with nothing happening to the believer as he comes to faith. His legal state and relation to God actually changes, in the Spirit's working of faith, from one of wrath to one of righteousness. Both abuses—extending objective justification to individuals and denying objective justification—are due to overreaches of human logic. Reason wants to simplify the both/and presentation of justification in Scripture into only a present act or only a past act. Both errors minimize the Gospel, one by conditioning it, and the other by making it old news.

The present power of the Gospel is due to the justification of the world in Christ—sin is actually paid for, and the declaration of Christ's justification in our place goes out to all in the Gospel. Conversion, as a present effect of an already present forgiveness in Christ, does not change God. It *does* change the sinner, though. Without any emphasis on the objectivity of justification, completed in Christ, man must be

---

[32]Martin Franzmann, "Reconciliation and Justification," 83.
[33]Joshua Sullivan, "Objective Justification: Part Two."

the determining factor that effects a change in God's relationship to men, one believer at a time. Faith, in this scheme, cannot help but be propitiatory. Faith, then, effects salvation, which is incomplete until each person individually comes along with the missing ingredient: faith.

However, we must be equally diligent not to blithely think that any definition of objective justification will do. Words regarding an individual's justification, like "saint," should be reserved for the personal aspect of justification, which is by faith. "It is better, however, not to use the word 'impart' of the universal justification of the world, because in our German language it almost always signifies not only a presenting from God's side, but also an accepting from man's side."[34] Imputation, as a theological word, designates possession. All such "receiving" words are best not used with the universal aspect of Christ' work and benefits. The individual appropriation of what God offers is by faith. We must be careful in our language and definitions, distinguishing between words that are used only in a universal sense and those used in an individual sense, to keep the scriptural teaching solid, lest Satan have a field day among us, as he is currently.

---

[34]Walther, *Justification—Objective and Subjective*, 18.

Chapter 12

Objective Justification: Law and Gospel Kiss in Christ

The modern debate over justification concerns the effect of the atonement. Objective justification describes the "worldwide effect or consequence of Christ's vicarious (substitutionary) obedience."[1] It answers the question: Did it change anything from God's side of the relationship? As detailed last chapter, wrath and justification are both valid and essential—one outside of Christ and one in Christ. In Christ we find the meeting point of these two judgments.

Christ died as a sinner under the law, and yet He rose without sin. The same is true of man: humanity is both righteous and sinful, from God's viewpoint. The Gospel speaks what is true in Christ, and the law speaks as if there is no forgiveness. In Christ, the totality of man is forgiven and already righteous, yet because sinners are in Adam from birth, they are complete heirs of hell, fully under God's condemnation. "In Christ" is representative language—it cannot be assumed true outside of Christ. "If I do not have Christ, then I do not have my justification. If I remain in this Christless state until I die, then I die a lost man, dead in trespasses and sins, under the wrath and condemnation of God, and

---

[1]Maier, "A Summary Exposition of Justification," 11.

without hope."[2] As the Gospel is universal and objectively true before man hears it, so is the law: "Just as the Law teaches Universal Objective Damnation, so the Gospel teaches Universal Objective Justification."[3]

Only in the person of Christ—in His substitutionary death and resurrection—can it be said that God's wrath is eradicated and sin destroyed. "This foreign righteousness is such that the payment of guilt and the complete obedience of the Law satisfied divine wrath."[4] This is why the Gospel "can't be placed in conjunction with the Law in a way completely satisfying to our human reason and logic."[5] Fleshly reason can only consider the state of affairs outside of Christ, apart from the promise. The cross of Christ and His sacrifice makes no sense without God's wrath, yet the law still brings wrath to this day (Rom. 4:15). The law Christ was born under—the verdict over our sins—cursed Him to death. Yet, the Lord also rose victorious over sin, so we, in Christ, have victory over the whole world. "Whoever believes in the Son has eternal life; whoever does not obey the Son shall not see life, but the wrath of God remains on him" (Jn. 3:36).

As the Gospel does not undo the law, so the wrath of God cannot be used against forgiveness. Rom. 5 speaks of the two coordinating verdicts that Christ gave in the dual power of the keys. Both powers, to bind and to loose, are in effect and are valid verdicts before God in heaven. Outside of Christ, all are condemned, while in Christ there is only righteousness and God's justification for sinners.

Law and Gospel meet in Christ, the holy God who "became sin." However, the righteous Savior does not merely *make* a payment, He *is* the payment, the very Lamb of God. "And having been perfected, He became the author of eternal salvation to all who obey Him" (Heb. 5:9). He does not remain in the tomb, but is vindicated and absolved of sin—our sin. It is the height of absurdity and foolishness that damnation, hell, and sin are found only in God and that He physically died and was absolved for the world. Yet, that is the truth. There is only wrath and death outside of Christ, but there is only justification—and no wrath

---

[2] David Jay Webber, "Our Righteousness before God," 50.

[3] Martin Diers, "Objective Justification," 15.

[4] Martin Chemnitz, *Loci Theologici*, quoted in: Robert Preus, "Justification as Taught by Post-Reformation Lutheran Theologians," 12.

[5] Rick Curia, *History of Objective or Universal Justification*, 34.

for anyone—in Christ.

Reason wants to simplify the matter for itself and make the divine truth more palatable: God's "verdict is: life for believers, condemnation for unbelievers."[6] If there is no overlap of law and Gospel, though, man's response must be the cause of the switchover. The Gospel cannot do it if there is no forgiveness or justification before faith. Reason always gravitates to the law, ignoring the true freedom that exists in Christ. In ways that are both subtle and crass, human reason asserts that Christ is not the justifier of mankind:

> We doubt whether it is scientifically correct to say that the Resurrection of Christ is the formal cause of God's justifying, but if one single man since Christ's Resurrection, whether by falling away or otherwise, is actually not justified, that is quite enough to prove that the fact of Christ's Resurrection is not the formal cause of man's being justified.[7]

Reason struggles with the promise of grace because it sees and feels only sin and condemnation. It wants the Word to match its experience. In the words of the Confessions: the "whole system is derived either from human reason or from the teaching of the law rather than the Gospel."[8] The tendency to make the Gospel simple or clear to sinful man must be an attempt to redefine it in law terms, to make God's wrath a greater reality than forgiveness in Christ.

The dual verdicts create a limbo for man, centered in the person of Christ. Sin is to be condemned, and faith is to be preached to all, regardless of the audience. "It is hard for human reason to believe that if God has forgiven He can still condemn."[9] When more carefully phrased, no contradiction exists: God forgave in Christ, and those in Adam are condemned, but man looks at the state of affairs from his point of view, and not from Christ's: "If with Christ you died to the elemental spirits of the world, why, as if you were still alive in the world, do you submit to regulations . . . " (Col. 2:20). Man's final state cannot be both in

---

[6]Paul Rydecki, blog comment on "Luther's Translation of 2 Corinthians 5:19."

[7]"Smith's Inquiry Into Catholic Truths," review of Charles Smith, *An Inquiry into the Catholic Truths hidden under certain Articles of the Creed of the Church of Rome*, 2 vols., in *The Theologian and Ecclesiastic* X (London: Joseph Masters, 1850; http://play.google.com/books/reader?id=0CkEAAAAQAAJ), 162.

[8]Ap 4:287, quoted in: Martim Warth, "Justification through Faith in Article Four of the Apology," 108.

[9]Siegbert Becker, "Objective Justification," 14.

Christ and in Adam, so the result must be either eternal salvation or eternal damnation. Forgiveness is centered in God's cursing of Christ, who became a curse Himself (Gal. 3:13). Outside of Christ's death, there is only more death—not justification and life. Jesus was not acting independently of us in His rising from our death: He "represented us all and acted on our part before God."[10] The price Jesus paid—Himself—is the same body the Father raised in vindication. "Apart from Christ [God] sees us as guilty sinners, in and through Christ [He] now considers us to be not guilty because of the atoning work of the Savior."[11] As Rom. 5 teaches: "In both cases sin and righteousness exist as realities prior to the individual lives affected by them."[12]

How does eliminating (the theological significance of) the resurrection, and its effects, change the Gospel? It causes one to " 'legalize' the Gospel by making it a message of conditional forgiveness, even if 'faith' is the only condition left to make forgiveness a reality for the individual."[13] This is where we would be with a dead (to us) Christ, who did not rise for us: "And thus strictly regarded, the death of Jesus, according to Paul, has not so much reconciled humanity with God, as it has removed the obstacles to the reconciliation."[14] The possibility for God to be reconciled at some point is not a message of reconciliation which gives the justification for which Jesus was raised.

Luther did not preach a conditional message in which God was waiting for man's response to take away sin:

> This [proclaimed forgiveness] signifies nothing else than that the Gospel should be preached, which declares unto all the world that in Christ the sins of all the world are swallowed up, and that he suffered death to put away sin from us, and arose to devour it, and blot it out. All this he did, that whoever believeth, should have the comfort and assurance that it is reckoned unto him, even as if he himself had done it. . . . [15]

---

[10] John Jacob Rambach (1693–1735), quoted in: Rick Curia, *History of Objective or Universal Justification*, 28.

[11] Siegbert Becker, "Objective Justification," 7.

[12] Tom Hardt, "Justification and Easter," 53.

[13] Rick Curia, *History of Objective or Universal Justification*, 8.

[14] Heinrich Meyer, *Hand-book to the Epistles to the Corinthians*, 535.

[15] Sermon for Easter Tuesday, *Complete Sermons of Martin Luther*, 1.2:316.

The dual effects of the two originators—Adam and Christ—are both present realities, but human logic may not extend or change either one. We dare not say that all individuals are justified. Neither can it be said that all individuals are damned because the whole world in Adam is condemned. Nor may we say that God's condemnation is more powerful than the justification for all proceeding from Christ. Both powers are equally valid.[16] "The verdict of 'not-guilty' was pronounced once for all by God upon the world in Christ, its substitute."[17] What happened to Christ in His rising is just as much ours as our sins were His in His death: "His life is our life; his pardon, our pardon; his justification, our justification."[18] In contrast, if faith justifies in place of Christ, the Father needs more from man to be placated. Faith ends up needing to complete the work of Christ. One consistent denier of objective justification claims that "justification was the result of Abraham's faith."[19] But if Abraham did something, even in not rejecting faith, to gain justification, then his faith would be a work, something to boast about. "For if Abraham was justified by works, he has something to boast about, but not before God" (Rom. 4:2).

The logical contradiction of coordinating wrath and forgiveness outside of Christ is a burden to fallen reason. Rydecki said to a defender of objective justification, "you can label the teaching of justification by faith alone in Christ a perversion."[20] The real reason he claims objective justification makes faith unnecessary is that man, in totality, is both justified universally and condemned universally, and that does not make sense to man and his thinking. Another denier of the objective aspect expects a simple, one-sided answer: "If objective justification doesn't really remove the wrath of God and save the sinner from eternal condemnation until and unless faith is added, then it is no

---

[16]"Both acts [Adam's and Christ's] have an equally general signification and validity. But as not all men are personally condemned, although the 'judgment came upon all men to condemnation,' so not all men are really and personally justified, although the justification has through Christ's act 'come upon all men'." Quoted in: Tom Hardt, "Justification and Easter," 75.

[17]Jon Buchholz, "Jesus Canceled Your Debt!," 26.

[18]Walther, Easter Sermon, quoted in: Rick Curia, *History of Objective or Universal Justification*, 25.

[19]Paul Rydecki, "Francis Pieper's Misuse of Romans 4:25," 8.

[20]Paul Rydecki, blog comment on "Luther's Translation of 2 Corinthians 5:19."

justification at all."[21] This is the Calvinist seduction, applied to the fruit of the atonement, rather than to the atonement itself. If Christ justified all in His own rising, then all must be justified eventually, so reason thinks, but Scripture, and therefore God Himself, does not operate with such simplistic if/then logic. If faith and salvation coexist in a simple cause and effect relationship, then man is under wrath and God is not reconciled until he believes. Christ, as our mediator, becomes a mere prelude to forgiveness. This idea attributes all to faith in time, making God in Christ the preamble to salvation, rather than the source and basis for all justification.

Our sins necessitated Christ's reception into God's favor. Christ was our surety, acting for us and assuming our position before God.

> The suretyship of Christ is presupposed, and the argument is: Since He occupied the place of His people, and took their responsibilities, they are justified in their representative, and no more in their sins. Not only so; redeemed humanity, raised from the dead in their living Head, and having life judicially awarded to it, cannot be holden of corruption, in soul or in body; for their whole persons are redeemed, and indissolubly united to Him. But it is premial [accorded as a reward] life.[22]

This description of Christ as our surety is a traditional way of emphasizing a critical point: "So Christ—our Divine Sponsor and Proxy—died, not only for the good of Mankind, but in the place of Mankind."[23] Christ became sin, not merely the one paying the debt or incurring the fine of sin. Forgiveness—our life—is not disconnected from the glorified body of the Son who rose on Easter. He was raised in our place, becoming our justification.

The debt for sin Christ assumed, and the payment He made, was ours. "For the love of Christ controls us, because we have concluded this: that one has died for all, therefore all have died" (2 Cor. 5:14). The debt of sin—our guilt—was discharged when Christ was resurrected by the Father. Christ's life is, in a real sense, our life: "as Christ was raised

---

[21] Vernon Harley, "Synergism—Its Logical Association with General Justification."

[22] George Smeaton, *The Doctrine of the Atonement as Taught by Christ Himself*, 186.

[23] Chr. Wordsworth, *The New Testament of Our Lord and Saviour Jesus Christ, in the Original Greek: with Notes and Introductions: St. Paul's Epistles* (London: Rivingtons, 1872; http://books.google.com/books?id=QOMsAAAAYAAJ), 172.

from the dead by the glory of the Father, even so we also should walk in newness of life" (Rom. 6:4). Christ's life is not less real or effective than death in Adam. The results of His work are not less universal than Adam's first sin, and neither is the Gospel less real, objective, and universal than the law. Of course, the reception is very different: one is to be believed, while the other is propagated naturally.

The clash of law and Gospel is complete only in Christ, resolving the verdict of Adam, but to make law and Gospel simple, coordinating partners outside of Christ—taking turns one at a time—is to lose both: "Christian doctrine is one congruent message, with no contradictions."[24] But there are many difficulties from man's view. This apparent contradiction between objective justification and subjective justification allows for the proclamation of a universal Gospel to all mankind, which does not militate against the law—the call for all to repent of their sins. Objective justification does not undo justification by faith any more than the general condemnation in Adam prevents calling out people's specific sins.

There is no contradiction between what happens in Christ at His resurrection and what happens in time during the preaching act. Both the law and the Gospel are to be applied as realities, so people are preached into Christ, where there is no sin, but only righteousness. Wrath is no more in Christ: God is fully satisfied with the sacrifice of Christ, to whom our sins were imputed. Christ's righteousness is given and received in the Gospel, but it is imputed, and we benefit from it, in faith.

> We are given God's verdict in this Word, which changes our status before Him. We cannot believe in what we do not know for sure. Sure and certain forgiveness gives rise to faith. This forgiveness is rooted in the cross and the resurrection, the verdict of absolution given to the world. If Christ had not absolved (forgiven) the world of sins, the Word which delivers that forgiveness would be null and void. This is the teaching of objective justification, which tells us that the Gospel can be applied to all people.[25]

Luther instructs us:

---

[24] Gregory Jackson, *Luther versus the Pietists*, 61.

[25] Philip Hale, *A Doctrinal Exposition of Galatians: A Sermonic Commentary for Laymen* (Omaha, NE: Mercinator Press, 2018), 109.

> But the true theology teaches that there is no more sin in the world, because Christ, on whom, according to Is. 53:6, the Father has laid the sins of the entire world, has conquered, destroyed, and killed it in His body. Having died to sin once, He has truly been raised from the dead and will not die anymore. Therefore wherever there is faith in Christ, there sin has in fact been abolished, put to death, and buried. But where there is no faith in Christ, there sin remains.[26]

Objective justification connects Christ's work to the mass of sinners in the Gospel. It is the cornerstone of forgiveness, the most important power in the world: Christ's key to heaven.

---

[26]"Lectures on Galatians" (1535), LW 26:286.

Chapter 13

The Most Dangerous Doctrine

As in all satanic controversies, there is now much popular propaganda being fed to unsuspecting laity. Any version of objective justification is called an inherent denial of justification by faith. This is simply a lie, which is why no evidence has been brought forth. For a supposed heresy that is said to be at least 150 years old, there should be plenty of false statements to expose.

ELDoNA implores people to leave churches holding to objective justification.[1] That this warning is directed at their former church bodies, in which they were educated, should not be ignored.[2] It is personal, but also differentiates them from their mother churches, no doubt. "Objective justification is not the truth of the Gospel,"[3] or as another author claims, objective justification is "the only important doctrine to the old synodical conference."[4] This is clearly a foolish, irrational attack, as if churches taught and defended nothing else. But

---

[1] Youtube documentary, "Justification Made Clear."

[2] It was admitted that what they were taught was not understood: "Indeed; until the issue was pressed, we reckoned the reasoning of Dr. Marquart and the Ft. Wayne faculty to be sound, that there was just an issue of bad terminology that could be overcome by simply refraining from using terms beyond those of Scripture and the Confessions." Eric Stefanski, "Theses on the Article of Justification: A Refutation of the ACLC's Critique: Part 9."

[3] Joshua Sullivan, Youtube documentary, "Justification Made Clear."

[4] Gregory Jackson, *Luther versus the Pietists*, 11.

the charge, which is leveled without actual examples of abuse, is a most serious one: "They destroy the Gospel."[5]

The phrase "justification by faith" sounds especially Lutheran, but these words are not a doctrine or full-bodied teaching. This phrase is used against Christ in the modern denial of objective justification. Faith and Christ go together, but "faith alone," evidently for some, excludes Christ's work of applying forgiveness. If God is not reconciled, so that Christ's atonement is not received, acknowledged, and applied to mankind by the Father, the Gospel itself is a lie. The result is that God is not at peace with man—He is only wrathful. But Scripture speaks otherwise: "Glory to God in the highest, and on earth peace among those with whom he is pleased!" (Lk. 2:14). "For in him all the fullness of God was pleased to dwell, and through him to reconcile to himself all things, whether on earth or in heaven, making peace by the blood of his cross" (Col. 1:20). Through Christ, nothing exists that is not reconciled, so every repentant sinner may be forgiven.

The deniers of objective justification do argue against a real abuse. However, in their overzealousness, they rip all comfort from the Gospel. They safeguard the Gospel so much that it is removed from this world and placed in heaven, not in churches and human mouths. What are they preaching, though, if not forgiveness?

In avoiding one extreme, the deniers of objective justification marry themselves to another and become no better than the "evangelical" Christian, with his acceptance language and sinner's prayer. Though one is dressed up in more biblical language and pious Lutheran phrases, both see salvation completed in man, as faith must do what Christ left undone. The Lutheran Confessions, however, speak correctly to man's role in conversion:

> Concerning the righteousness of faith before God we believe, teach, and confess unanimously, in accordance with the comprehensive summary of our faith and confession presented above, that poor sinful man is justified before God, that is, absolved and declared free and exempt from all his sins, and from the sentence of well-deserved condemnation, and adopted into sonship and heirship of eternal life, without any merit or worth of our own, also without any preceding, present, or any subsequent works, out of pure grace, because

---

[5]Gregory Jackson, *Luther versus the Pietists*, 61.

of the sole merit, complete obedience, bitter suffering, death, and resurrection of our Lord Christ alone, whose obedience is reckoned to us for righteousness (FC SD 3:9).

The righteousness of faith is not *because* of faith, but flows from what Christ has already done. It comes to sinners in the absolution, which is nothing but the Gospel. There are no unfulfilled aspects of this righteousness in Christ.

One ELDoNA pastor, after ridiculing objective justification, makes the plea: "find a church that does not teach this."[6] However, what this propaganda fails to articulate is that almost all churches deny that justification has a universal and an objective aspect. Liberal churches deny this because they have no justification—neither the objective nor subjective element—to defend. They do not even hold to the sanctity of life, as delineated in the fifth commandment, let alone the necessity of repentance and faith. The large, liberal Evangelical Lutheran Church in America (ELCA) denies objective justification. In fact, many of its predecessor bodies directly opposed the Missouri Synod on this exact issue during the time of Walther, Pieper, and Engelder. In 1888 "a new peak [occurred] in the controversy over the doctrine of objective justification, this time primarily between Missouri and her former ally, [the] Ohio [Synod], who joined the attack on Missouri begun by [the] Iowa [Synod]."[7] Later, "Ohio's Richard Charles Henry Lenski (1864–1936) ridiculed the fact that Missouri taught" objective justification.[8] In denying the fullness of the Gospel, there was little foundation left on which to fight the external issues of morality and basic scriptural facts.

In the 1870s, the more liberal General Council took the side of the Augustana and Iowa synods, rejecting the teaching of general justification promoted by the Norwegian and Missouri synods, along with the Evangelical Lutheran Synodical Conference of North America.[9] These General Council churches, which rejected Missouri on this very issue, are now part of the ELCA. The fruit of this denial is now plain to see, unlike the baseless charges made against objective justification today.

Gottfried Fritschel (1836–1889) of the Iowa Synod, a professor at

---

[6] Joshua Sullivan, "Objective Justification: Part 4."
[7] Rick Curia, *History of Objective or Universal Justification*, 48.
[8] Rick Curia, *History of Objective or Universal Justification*, 33.
[9] Rick Curia, *History of Objective or Universal Justification*, 29.

Wartburg College, had the same playbook as those who now deny objective justification. Fritschel made the "charge that the teaching of objective justification robbed 'subjective' justification of its forensic nature on God's part." He played justification by faith against its basis, and called objective justification "apostasy from the Lutheran doctrine of justification."[10] Either Fritschel was ignorant, or he "simply wanted to use this controversy to take some shots at the Missouri Synod."[11] The same rings true today as was said in 1872 of the Iowa Synod, "That they care more about the fighting than about the thing itself."[12]

The polemics surrounding this issue, both now and stretching back over a century, have been quite bitter, and at times, irrational. It is nothing new: "The 'hue and cry' raised against objective justification— in essence, if not in name—in 1888 and 1905 and 1933, at Kokomo, Indiana, in 1979 and at present in 1982, is the same raised in 1864 and 1871."[13] That does not mean there is not an issue of substance worth fighting for. This unseemly and unchurchly conduct occurred also during the doctrinal controversies that necessitated the *Formula of Concord* in the 16th century: "there was a disputation not only concerning the words, but the doctrine itself was attacked in the most violent manner, and it was contended that the new obedience in the regenerate is not necessary because of the above-mentioned divine order" (FC SD 4:5).

---

[10]Quoted in: Rick Curia, *History of Objective or Universal Justification*, 30, 35.

[11]Rick Curia, *History of Objective or Universal Justification*, 30.

[12]Walther, *Justification—Objective and Subjective*, 22.

[13]Rick Curia, *History of Objective or Universal Justification*, 35.

Chapter 14

The One-Sided, Anachronistic Charge of Huberianism

This is the logic of dismissing objective justification without actually considering it: If justification by faith is not the only way to talk of justification, then there is a justification outside of faith, so that (all) individuals are justified apart from faith. In addition to its poor logic, this approach is not actually a position of those who teach an objective aspect of justification. The assumption is that the absolution in Christ cancels out the verdict of condemnation—resulting in universalism—so that everyone is saved, ruling out individual justification and conversion. That leads to another dishonest charge—that of "Huberianism." Today this is a frequent accusation. It is named after the quasi-Lutheran Samuel Huber (1547–1624), "a largely insignificant and forgotten figure in history."[1] This minor figure taught a new doctrine that was widely condemned in his time. So, why has he been resurrected in modern debates on justification?

Both Huber and his teaching were soundly condemned by orthodox Lutherans during his time, but the charge of "Huberianism" has become something of a battle cry for modern deniers of objective justification. This is quite odd, because this man's error was peculiar and insignificant,

---

[1] ACLC, "Critique of ELDoNA," 30.

though there is some similarity in terminology. He was no Arius seducing many, nor has anyone promoted him or his work in a positive way to publicly support objective justification. Yet, the charge is made without a witness. "Any assertion that Walther's teaching of universal objective justification as a continuation of Huber's heresies is either ignorant or dishonest."[2] In fact, Huber taught a novel doctrine, unlikely to be duplicated again.

It is the deniers of the objective aspect of justification who talk incessantly of "Huberianism," writing and publishing about him.[3] At times the charge is merely insinuated:

> We ought not think that Walther (and Schaller and Hoe-necke), Pieper, [and others], who formulated the current expressions of "Objective Justification" were unfamiliar with either Huber or Aegidius Hunnius [Huber's orthodox opponent]. The question is how dependent upon Huber they were, since they specifically distanced themselves from him. That is, did they see themselves as accidentally using the same terminology or did they intentionally adopt it while seeking to remove the parts of his teaching that they knew were offensive and keep the rest?[4]

This moves the argument back in time, as if it were a neatly settled debate today:

> This common outline, this "justification by faith alone in Christ" was the only concept of justification espoused by the Lutherans in the age of orthodoxy. No other justification was known in the Lutheran Church—until Samuel Huber (1547–1624) arrived on the scene.[5]

If modern proponents can be simply identified, in a back-handed way, with a long defeated errorist, the argument is implicitly won without considering what is actually being taught.

Very little is definitely said about Huber today, since neither he, nor his writings are well-known. He is mainly known from the minor writings of his orthodox opponents. While Huber taught a universal justification, it was not limited by a teaching of subjective justification

---

[2] Jon Buchholz, "Jesus Canceled Your Debt!," 24.

[3] Aegidius Hunnius, *Theses Opposed to Huberianism: A Defense of the Lutheran Doctrine of Justification,* trans. Paul A. Rydecki (Createspace Independent Publishing Platform, 2012).

[4] ELDoNA, "Theses on the Article of Justification," 10.

[5] Paul Rydecki, "The Forensic Appeal to the Throne of Grace," 17.

or keeping the verdict "in Christ." One writing of Huber is entitled: "The Invincible Truth Concerning the Election and Predestination of the Human Race to Eternal Life, Accomplished by Christ Jesus."[6] Huber taught something much more than the objective link between Christ's resurrection and the justification of believers by faith.

By all accounts, Huber overreacted against the limited atonement of Calvinism.[7] He is also rejected by modern proponents of objective justification, since his error involved election, not simply the basis for justification. "Huber views election as God's earnest desire that all people would be saved and as the call to all people to come to faith in Christ. This is how he is able to say that God 'elected' all people, even though this is not how Scripture uses that word."[8] In Huber's own words:

> Therefore, I confess that he secretly abandoned and passed over no one in his counsel, just as he also gave all people to his Son and through him sought and desired the salvation and blessedness of all people. Therefore, by this I confess also, just as Paul says in Ephesians 1, "God chose us before the beginning of the world through Christ, that we should be holy and blameless," that for such a purpose he chose and elected through this his Son not only some, not only a few, not only a select part. But just as Christ is a universal Savior and came into the world to save sinners and came to give life to the world, that we might live holy, blessed, and eternal lives, so also God elected and ordained through his Son all sinners, that is, all people to life, salvation and blessedness.[9]

Those who make the charge of "Huberianism" have not shown how modern uses of the term "objective justification" deal with election at all, or that it proclaims unbelievers "were foreseen, ordained and elected by God through his dear Son."[10] Huber is a very distracting red herring in the objective justification debate.

---

[6]"Samuel Huber on Election and Justification: Translations from His Writings," trans. Andrew Hussman (April 26, 2013; http://essays.wls.wels.net/bitstream/handle/123456789/2282/Huber%20Translations_0.pdf), 20.

[7]"Therefore, let us meet this Calvinism with the power and grace of God, and let us also expose its deceits everywhere and confound it through the word of God." "Samuel Huber on Election and Justification," 10.

[8]Andrew Hussman, "Samuel Huber on Election and Justification," 2.

[9]"Samuel Huber on Election and Justification," 12.

[10]"Samuel Huber on Election and Justification," 13.

Mentioning Huber, and his condemnation centuries ago, is guilt by (terminological) association: "Our old dogmaticians too would themselves have used the expression ['the world is justified'] more—since they believed and taught the substance—had not Huber shortly before Gerhard's time taught that God had not only justified all men already, but had also elected them to eternal life."[11] Huber was his own man with his own errors, but in a careful teaching of justification, " 'Objective justification' does not deprive 'subjective justification' of its 'objective' reality. It is possible that the terms can be abused in that direction, and the appropriateness of the terminology can always be discussed."[12]

Huber taught a version of universal justification, though, "We must not condemn by the application of labels, but must address what is actually taught or not taught by any party."[13] After all, it is not a sin to use new words or even ones that have been abused in the past. To mandate such a thing would severely limit what could be said. Here, the extreme legalism of those Lutherans who deny the Gospel and its objective basis is felt most forcefully.

While a heavy emphasis on objective justification might sound like universalism to some, we can look to how Huber was denied: The first of the *Theses Opposed to Huberianism* reads:

> Huber professes such a justification, for the sake of which Christ has properly, actually and practically conferred redemption on the entire human race in such a way that sins have been equally remitted to all men, including the Turks, and that all men (including unbelievers) have received remission of sins, and that the whole human race has, in actual fact, been received into the grace and bosom of God.[14]

The words "conferred" and "received" refer to the subjective aspect of justification. In other words, Huber taught that the righteousness of Christ was imparted and imputed to unbelievers, not just declared in Christ and valid in the Gospel. But all good definitions of objective justification also leave room for the subjective or personal side of justification. Objective justification is not a standalone doctrine, though

---

[11] Walther, *Justification—Objective and Subjective*, 20.

[12] Tom Hardt, "Justification and Easter," 66.

[13] ACLC, "Critique of ELDoNA," 8.

[14] Paul Rydecki, "Comparing Huberianism and Lutheranism on Justification, Part 1" (Feb. 6, 2013; http://www.intrepidlutherans.com/2013/02/comparing-huberianism-and-lutheranism.html).

this duality is ignored by those who oppose it. This personal aspect of justification is indicated by the actual reception of forgiveness, not just the offer and declaratory act of Christ's resurrection from our death. To deniers of objective justification, however, there is only one possible meaning and aspect to justification, so they conflate the giving and receiving of the verdict, unable to distinguish between them. That is why the theses of Hunnius against Huber do nothing for the modern debate; they speak to a different issue.

Walther rejected the substance of what Huber taught. Huber used subjective justification words to speak of his objective justification, making it the only justification: "Christ imparted the redemption to the entire human race in the proper sense." The "imparted" word Huber used "refers to the appropriation," that is, not just what happened in Christ, but what happens in man.[15] This is explicitly rejected by Walther, who reserves the impartation of justification—man's possession of the righteous verdict—for faith: "It is better, however, not to use the word 'impart' (darreicht) of the universal justification of the world, because in our German language it almost always signifies not only a presenting (Darreichen) from God's side, but also an accepting from man's side."[16] Walther clearly had a more nuanced doctrine of justification than Huber, preserving both the objective and subjective aspects. He further suggests: "In order to avoid the appearance of agreement with this erroneous doctrine [of Huber], [the orthodox dogmaticians] used the expression [of world justification] rarely."[17]

What the modern charge of "Huberianism" shows is a grave logical error in those who cast it; careless opponents of any objective dimension to justification deny the duality of forgiveness. They flatten the entire issue, in both aspects, in their minds. For example: "Those who have not received the Gospel promises in faith remain condemned under the wrath of God;"[18] "only those will be justified who have faith in Jesus Christ, while those who do not believe in Jesus remain under God's wrath."[19] While these phrases sound orthodox when used of individuals,

---

[15] Walther, *Justification—Objective and Subjective*, 20.

[16] Walther, *Justification—Objective and Subjective*, 18.

[17] Walther, *Justification—Objective and Subjective*, 20.

[18] Gregory Jackson, *Luther versus the Pietists*, 114.

[19] Gottfried Fritschel, quoted in: Rick Curia, *History of Objective or Universal Justification*, 30.

if true of all of mankind, there is no real grace—the forgiveness of a reconciled God—until one believes. This is a basic confusion of law and Gospel.

Faith does not change God, nor does it make the Gospel valid for select believers. This is the error of a subjective-only justification, which has more in common with the one-sided Huber than the carefully nuanced objective/subjective distinction. God's justification of the world in Christ does not nullify the universal condemnation of those in Adam: "A person, born and conceived in sin, is a child of wrath before he comes to faith. Yet, on the other hand, he is also a part of the reconciled world, which God loves, and therefore himself also reconciled to God and justified by God. This is not contradictory. It is a double approach to the same object."[20] The opponents of objective justification are so blinded in their zeal, they cannot consider what is said—only what they want to hear. That is why they try to make this modern fight a 16th century debate and legislate what particular words are kosher for orthodox Lutherans today.

Due to new errors, which always present themselves, the orthodox explanation of Scripture becomes more refined over time. To highlight the objective benefits of Christ in the subjective cesspool of modern evangelicalism, it is most helpful to view man both in Christ and outside of Christ. This is simply the twin powers of the law and the Gospel. Both may be applied at any time to any person, because both are objectively true. Faith does not flip the switch on God's wrath, as an atoning propitiation. Neither does it replace the keys Christ actually gave to the Church.

Despite similarities in language to Huber, or whatever inconsistencies in vocabulary manifest themselves, the real issue is not words, but what is actually being said. Pieper summarizes Walther's teaching quite clearly: "Thus the whole world has been justified through the resurrection of Christ. With this the fact that man is justified by faith in no way stands in contradiction, for when we speak of faith the personal appropriation on the part of man and the imputation of the righteousness which has been won on the part of God is emphasized."[21]

---

[20] George Stoeckhardt, "[Yet a Word Concerning Justification]," *Lehre und Wehre* 35, quoted in: Rick Curia, *History of Objective or Universal Justification*, 55.

[21] F. Pieper, "Walther as Theologian: Justification, Universal," 3.

To play these aspects against each other will undo all Christian teaching. Christ tells us how these disparate powers of the law and the Gospel are to be used: the unrepentant are not to be encouraged by the Gospel and the repentant are not to be beat down to hell by the law. So also in justification, we must avoid all Huberian excesses, thinking justification is only objective or only subjective.

Chapter 15

Gospel Receptionism

Simply stated, the whole debate on justification today may be summed up in one question: What does the Gospel deliver to the unbeliever? The denial of objective justification parallels the error in the Lord's Supper, in which the body and blood of Christ are said to be present, but only insofar as the believer and his faith make it so. In the Supper, the question of what it is must be separated from faith, so the determining demarcation is: What does the unbeliever receive? Does the one without faith receive Christ's body and blood, or merely bread and wine? So, also with objective justification, the question is: What does the unbeliever receive in the proclamation of the true Gospel?

The objective aspect of justification defines the Gospel most accurately, because it brackets off man's response entirely. Objective justification confesses, most basically, that "forgiveness exists already *prior* to faith, as its object."[1] If faith is the power that actually saves, rather than the Gospel, which delivers what is available in Christ, what is the Gospel? It merely points to a possible forgiveness without offering it. The objective approach to justification, before faith occurs, disconnects the issue entirely from faith. It does not deny that man is justified by faith alone, but it digs down to the more fundamental question of where forgiveness is realized—apart from any one individual.

The distinction within justification helps to show the true nature of not only the Gospel, but also faith. Is the Gospel a device without a

---

[1]Kurt Marquart, "Objective Justification," *Marquart's Works*, 6:72.

battery, that does nothing for us without faith—its engine—to power it? Is faith, in time, even as a gift and act of God, the power of the Gospel, or is forgiveness the direct result of Christ's redemptive actions? These are not theoretical questions—they are directly linked to who may speak the Gospel and how. Answers to these questions determine the nature of the forgiveness on which faith depends.

Objective justification speaks to the enacted reality of forgiveness, completed from God's side, so that "this treasure is also offered and presented to all in Word and Sacrament."[2] "Those who deny objective justification state that if we say that the sins of the world are already forgiven, then there is no longer any need for justifying faith."[3] But unless forgiveness is objectively tied to Christ's body, man will take the credit and assume he is the basis for it. Christ alone changed things for all people, so that God is now reconciled. This is not in regards to needing faith (man's side of things), but in God's relationship and attitude toward the world. Scripture attests to this:

> But now in Christ Jesus you who once were far off have been brought near by the blood of Christ. For he himself is our peace, who has made us both one and has broken down in his flesh the dividing wall of hostility by abolishing the law of commandments expressed in ordinances, that he might create in himself one new man in place of the two, so making peace, and might reconcile us both to God in one body through the cross, thereby killing the hostility (Eph. 2:13–16).

The blood of Christ, not the blood of faith, accomplishes the removal of God's hostility. This peace, "in himself," leads to faith and makes it possible. God is not far from us or wrathful—"in Christ Jesus," God is near and gracious, through His expiating blood.

To answer the question "What is the Gospel?" is also to state in what way Christ's work applies to the whole world. It delivers what, in Christ, was given and declared. If there is no basis for justification before and apart from faith, then there is only law—that is, God's anger and wrath at sin. Forgiveness is then eradicated absolutely. Faith, if objective justification is denied, becomes the lever to move God and make Him forgiving to man.

---

[2]Walther, *Justification—Objective and Subjective*, 41.
[3]Martin Diers, "Objective Justification," 7.

"Faith alone" does not show us what faith itself rests on. Faith is not an absolute principle or independent substance, since true faith is always in Christ and rests on His effective benefits. "Is the object of justifying faith the forgiveness of sins which Christ has already won for the world, or is it, rather, in the promise that God will forgive sins when the sinner believes that God is willing to do so?"[4] This promise of future forgiveness would make the Gospel a conditional opportunity for pardon—an offer with a string (of faith) attached, not the delivery of forgiveness itself. "God's promise to the sinner in his Word is that He will justify and save the sinner if and when the latter accepts Christ as his Redeemer from sin."[5] But if God is not forgiving towards mankind, but only wrathful, Christ's death and resurrection do not mark a change towards man; it is, rather, *his* acceptance of God that changes the whole state of affairs. Man, then, is what makes the Gospel true, not Christ.

If the Gospel is not itself absolution to all whom it is poured out upon, it is reduced to mere directions on how to get this as of yet absent forgiveness. But faith is not a string or condition God lays upon man, as a burden of the law. Faith is the reception and appropriation of what God has declared in Christ: all sin is forgiven and all sinners are now reconciled. "The sinner does not make a general salvation applicable to himself by faith; if that were true, salvation would not be complete before man performs the act of faith."[6] Here we see most clearly the modern Protestant error: man's response to the Gospel is more important than the Gospel of the living Christ. This is a reversal which turns the precious forgiveness of the Gospel into a curse of the law, all in the name of "faith." It is a most destructive error, even if it lurks in the garb of Lutheran phrases.

To remove faith from the foundational question of where forgiveness comes from, we must ask: What does the unbeliever (one without faith) receive in the Gospel? "Is God's justification only effected when an individual trusts the promise of forgiveness?"[7] This is what objective justification, as one side of the justification equation, seeks to answer. Justification is effective for all, since it resides, complete and whole, in

---

[4]Martin Diers, "Objective Justification," 6.

[5]Maier, "A Summary Exposition of Justification," 9.

[6]John Schaller, *Biblical Christology*, quoted in: Rick Curia, *History of Objective or Universal Justification*, 77.

[7]Jon Buchholz, "Jesus Canceled Your Debt!," 1.

the justified Christ. Christ did not merely make an off-hand payment for sinners—He assumed all sin, death, and condemnation upon Himself. So, also, He does not remain dead until we apply His sacrificial merit to the Father in faith, thereby completing His work when we accept Him. This error confuses our reception of Christ's forgiveness with the Father's acceptance and vindication of Christ's work on our behalf. Without God's objective reconciliation, completed in Christ, man must try to do the impossible: "love a wrathful, judging, and punishing God" (Ap 4:36–37).

Objective justification defines how the reconciled Father views mankind in Christ. This objective fact of a gracious and non-wrathful God is the Gospel, which is for all to use: "faith, which freely receives the remission of sins, sets Christ, the Mediator and Propitiator, against God's wrath" (Ap 4:46). We do not set faith against God's wrath, as if personal faith is enough to satisfy His justice; rather, we use the justification that is objectively complete in Christ. This forgiveness is objectively available and applied to the hearer in the divine Gospel.

In the denial of objective justification, the Gospel has no power of its own, until the missing ingredient of faith is added. So, faith empowers this gospel, but it has no forgiveness, in itself, with which to justify. "Thus faith . . . brings into being something that was not there before, namely, the forgiveness of sins," as a meritorious cause.[8] So, in effect, Christ's work is ineffective and inert, without faith occurring in time. It is this final step of man's individual faith that completes salvation, doing what Christ was seemingly unable to do. This is not the Gospel of the Christ who rose victorious over sin. "God's forgiveness in Christ is not an inert 'pile of stuff,' waiting to be parceled out, or snatched by an act of human faith."[9] Forgiveness is not far off, but in the mouth of everyone speaking the Gospel.

What does the Gospel impart? This question ignores the state of affairs from man's side—the personal reception or appropriation. From God's vantage point, however, we must be able to deny that His forgiveness is dependent on the existence of faith in miserable sinners. All the world is viewed, in Christ, as justified. Because of this fact, sins are not imputed in Christ. In the Gospel proclamation, the power of

---

[8]George Stoeckhardt, "General Justification," 140.
[9]ACLC, "Critique of ELDoNA," 26.

Christ's resurrection is applied to the individual. The Gospel is not just a reminder of a past forgiveness, or the promise of future forgiveness, but a present divine word of absolution. To whomever this Gospel is communicated, it is a true forgiving of sins before God in heaven.

Objective justification isolates the power of the Gospel: "Neither by its power does the faith of the individual render the Evangelical promises which God pronounces in the Word of the Gospel or Absolution really valid, effectual and true. . . . "[10] If faith makes the Gospel true, and forgiveness is only found where there is faith, then for every individual outside of Christ "the means of grace only communicate a conditional promise of a forgiveness of sins that will take place if believed."[11] Christ and His justification are then contingent on faith—that is, man's response to the Gospel. The Gospel, in this accounting, is not good news of a gracious God—it only mentions the possibility of what God may do.

Justification is "objective because this [verdict in Christ] was God's unilateral act prior to and in no way dependent upon man's response to it."[12] If this is denied, the Gospel ceases to be a power and becomes an earthly offer of what we must do to obtain forgiveness. The "Gospel" is then a new law. "When used in connection with the article of justification, faith must always be regarded as receptivity."[13] Faith in no way completes or adds to justification.

Forgiveness in the Gospel may be compared to Baptism, which "is and remains a washing of rebirth no matter how many baptized people there are who have despised their baptismal grace."[14] A second Baptism is never needed, because the problem is never God's distribution of forgiveness in it, but man's actual rejection of it. As Luther taught, the power of Baptism is not dependent on faith, but derives its power from Christ: "Through Baptism he dedicates us to himself and imparts to us the power of his death and resurrection."[15] Baptism is, and remains, a

---

[10]Theses accepted at the first convention of the Synodical Conference (1872), quoted in: Rick Curia, *History of Objective or Universal Justification*, 37.

[11]Magnus Sørensen, "The Justification of Christ," 36.

[12]CTCR, "Theses on Justification," 12.

[13]CTCR, "Theses on Justification," 14.

[14]U.V. Koren, quoted in: Rick Curia, *History of Objective or Universal Justification*, 23.

[15]*Complete Sermons of Martin Luther*, 4.2:146.

true impartation of forgiveness. We dare not impute our wickedness of unbelief to God's seriousness in the presentation of forgiveness.

We may call the teaching that faith does not complete or enact the Gospel by any name. "Objective justification" has been used for a century and a half by Lutherans to emphasize the fact that faith does not satisfy God's wrath. It is not in any way comparable to Christ's death and subsequent acceptance. Faith is not a work which placates God's wrath, so there cannot be only wrath before the gracious announcement of God in Christ. Man's reception of Christ's benefits is not meritorious, earning or achieving something before the holy God. If forgiveness is incomplete in Christ, "then faith and conversion is made a meritorious cause of the forgiveness of sins and the doctrine of justification by grace for Christ's sake is overthrown."[16] The emphasis on the completed and universal reconciliation of God to the world safeguards this teaching of justification.

Those who want only to deal with the reception of the Gospel by individuals—the subjective aspect of justification—avoid one of the most hotly contested issues of our time. However, the basis for forgiveness and God's current relation to the world are primary matters in Christianity. Objective justification confesses the perfective completion of justification, and, therefore, forgiveness in the Gospel. Absolution in time is directly dependent on Christ. He bore all man's sin in death and was raised to victory in life, and so man's sins are taken away, in Christ, from the viewpoint of the Father. The Gospel is what is delivered to the unbeliever, who has no faith.

> Absolution is therefore also at all times valid and powerful in itself, for God therein declares Himself, through the mouth of His servant, as a God truly reconciled through Christ's blood and death, and thus distributes for His part the gift of forgiveness and righteousness to all, who are being absolved, although many do not become partakers of the gifts of grace proffered in the Gospel, on account of their unbelief.[17]

God's forgiving relationship to all mankind speaks of His reconciliation. The Gospel is grounded in the perfect reconciliation of God through Christ, just as the Supper is grounded on Christ's sure words—and not receiving it in faith. "The gospel is true before we believe it.

---

[16]F. Pieper, "Walther as Theologian: Justification, Universal," 1.

[17]Walther, *Justification—Objective and Subjective*, 31.

It does not become true when we believe it."[18] Our understanding of the Gospel—as either a real absolution or a treasure map to a hidden absolution—determines how it is used.

> The Gospel therefore is not a mere historical narrative of the accomplished work of the redemption, but much rather a powerful declaration of peace and a promise of grace on the part of God towards the world redeemed by Christ, and thus at all times a powerful means of grace, in which God for His part brings, proffers, distributes, gives and presents the forgiveness of sins and the righteousness acquired by Christ, even though not all to whom God issues His serious call of grace accept this invitation of the reconciled God, and thus also do not become partakers of the accompanying benefits.[19]

Faith, in the biblical sense, is defined by what it relies on. The "Absolution is an object for our faith and not a mere pointer to faith."[20] This is in accordance with the Word of God. Faith is caused by the Word of forgiveness, "So faith comes from hearing, and hearing through the word of Christ" (Rom. 10:17). What does faith cling to? Not to its own qualities, but to Christ, in whom there is true righteousness for all. Faith does not depend on itself as a reconciling virtue or power outside of Christ. The Gospel itself is a promise of forgiveness, a delivering and offering from God. The true Gospel, in whatever form it comes, is always absolution and forgiveness, whether it is received in faith or rejected in unbelief.

Faith, which is never perfected in man, is not an autonomous object without a basis more firm than itself. Deniers of objective justification resist the teaching that a completed product (forgiveness) is needed for faith to rest on: "one of the (false) philosophical principles consistently demanded by teachers of 'Objective Justification' [is] that there must be some pre-existing 'thing'—some action or event, rather than, simply, a promise (though we in the diocese hold that God's promise is as 'solid' as any person, action, event, or institution could be)."[21] Note the

---

[18]Rolf Preus, introduction to Herman Amberg Preus, "The Justification of the World," trans. Herbert Larson (1874; http://www.christforus.org/objectivejustification.htm).

[19]Thesis 7. Walther, *Justification—Objective and Subjective*, 30.

[20]Walther, *Justification—Objective and Subjective*, 33.

[21]Eric Stefanski, "Theses on the Article of Justification: A Refutation of the ACLC's Critique: Part 10."

radically different definition of "promise" used here, and that the Gospel is said to be nothing but the promise of God for something in the future. God promises forgiveness in the Gospel and actually delivers it through the same, since it is the power of God to open heaven. This definition above is like a mere human promise: one offers to do something in the future when a condition is met. This contrasts starkly with the fruit of Christ's justification of the world, as offered and presented in the Gospel. Only one viewpoint presents something on which faith may rest securely.

Without the finished reconciliation of God to mankind, there is a large gap between the atonement and justification, and the faith of believers becomes the bridge. Where is forgiveness found, and where does faith ascend to, if it is not actually delivered in the Gospel? According to one subjective-only explanation of justification: "On account of the satisfaction Christ made to the divine law, there exists, objectively, a Throne of Grace to which all sinners are invited (in the Gospel) to flee, an alternate place of judgment opened up as a result of God's grace and the obedience, suffering, death, and resurrection of Christ."[22] This righteous verdict itself, though, is not earthly or bound to the Gospel. It is directly caused and opened up by faith, to deniers of objective justification, so it is otherworldly. Faith transports one to this place where God is willing to be reconciled, while the Gospel is mere instructions on how to get there. "Discard this doctrine [of objective justification], and you will have to teach that men must supply the deficiency in Christ's work."[23] Forgiveness has nothing to do with the Gospel, if it only has to do with faith.

According to Rydecki: "Christ's death earned the justification of all sinners, so that anyone and everyone who enters God's courtroom believing in Christ is actually declared by God to be righteous."[24] "The justification of the sinner that only takes place as a result of a forensic appeal to the Throne of Grace."[25] But a full-bodied doctrine of the atonement includes its effect:

---

[22]Douglas Lindee, "Impressions from My Visit with ELDoNA at their 2013 Colloquium and Synod—PART V.4" (Jul. 9, 2013; http://www.intrepidlutherans.com/2013/07/impressions-from-my-visit-with-eldona_9.html).

[23]F. Pieper, *Christian Dogmatics*, 2:349–350.

[24]Paul Rydecki, "Francis Pieper's Misuse of Romans 4:25," 23.

[25]Paul Rydecki, "The Forensic Appeal to the Throne of Grace," 1.

> The Lord's Resurrection, the Christian's boast, the pledge
> of all our hope, is in a special sense the foundation of our
> religion, because it is the evidence that the atonement was
> at once complete and accepted. . . . This great fact was
> always viewed as connected in the closest manner with the
> expiation—necessarily distinguished from it, indeed, but not
> to be disjoined.[26]

The Gospel itself is the alternate judgment of God, the place where the resurrection righteousness of Christ is found. The Word has all we need. While the "Throne of Grace" is an old, simplistic Lutheran analogy, based on a Scripture verse (Heb. 4:16), it is not the only way to picture justification.

If the atonement did not actually change anything, it would be a small matter. Historically, the atonement included this objective aspect of justification, since they are so closely related. After all, an atonement that didn't accomplish anything of itself is not much of an atonement to be preached. Faith is not the final step in achieving salvation; rather, salvation is complete, and forgiveness for all is in Christ.

A Gospel promise with a condition, no matter how small, means Christ did not complete salvation, leaving it up to man to finish. If the reconciliation of God is incomplete, salvation is not on earth in the Gospel itself, but confined to "the Throne of Grace (*Gnadenthron*; i.e., the Mercy Seat, i.e., Christ), the 'new location' at which the sinner may be judged due to the Christ's bearing of all sin, rather than being judged at the seat of justice by the Law."[27] This oversimplifies the matter, leaving only the wrath of God in the law for sinners before faith. The Gospel is then somewhere else, not present and available everywhere in Christ and His Word. It cannot be relied upon, so that the kingdom of God would then be far away, not near (Matt. 3:2).

The Reformers and early Lutherans did use the "Mercy Seat" analogy, but, for modern deniers of objective justification, it loses it juridical and objective aspect. But that is exactly why they used it—to emphasize the judicial nature of justification. "The Throne of Grace, which is nothing other than Christ and His merit."[28] The essential question is,

---

[26] George Smeaton, *The Doctrine of the Atonement as Taught by Christ Himself*, 182.

[27] ELDoNA, "Theses on the Article of Justification," 4–5.

[28] ELDoNA, "Theses on the Article of Justification," 8.

when does the application of Christ's merit occur? Because Christ has been justified, it is in the Gospel, before faith, so faith can rely on it.

An inaccessible forgiveness that is never on earth without faith is not real forgiveness: "Regarding the proper object of faith: ought it be a pre-existing declaration/judicial pronouncement of forgiveness (without words) or the acquisition of a judicial pronouncement of forgiveness?"[29] But Christ's merit and a conditional gospel are not yet forgiveness: "the acquisition of God's declaration is not only the correct position, but that it provides that for which it is often asserted that 'Objective Justification' is necessary."[30] The earning, or "acquisition," of the justifying verdict is not the judgment of the Father, so it leaves God unreconciled.

The fundamental question is: Is the Gospel itself forgiveness—has the Father approved of mankind in Christ? The purchase price Christ paid must be accepted by the Father, discharging our debt. The problem for man's reason is that the Gospel is a universal word with universal validity. Without a divine acceptance of Christ's sacrifice, on man's behalf, God's relationship to the world is unchanged by Christ. "Holy Scripture does not teach that mankind is now seen as sinless apart from or prior to faith, but only that God's desire is to judge them through the Mercy Seat or Throne of Grace, which is Christ: those not so judged are still dead in their sins."[31] Speaking of sinners' subjective state does not address the more fundamental question of God's character in Christ. This desire to forgive is said to be equivalent to grace. But this forgiveness from God's side is said to not yet have come upon mankind, so faith must transport the believer to a hidden place where the justification to life is found; "justification occurs in the divine courtroom, not without the accused fleeing in faith to the Throne of Grace, not *before* the accused flees in faith to the Throne of Grace, but *simultaneously* with this 'fleeing' or this 'forensic appeal'."[32] "Fleeing" or "appealing," which should really be synonymous with faith, does something for God in this scheme. Faith makes the jump and completes the circuit of justification, since there is nothing, in their view, that justifies prior to faith.

---

[29] ELDoNA, "Theses on the Article of Justification," 9.

[30] ELDoNA, "Theses on the Article of Justification," 10.

[31] ELDoNA, "Theses on the Article of Justification," 11.

[32] Paul Rydecki, "The Forensic Appeal to the Throne of Grace," 5.

If faith does not rest on the already existing object of justification in Christ, forgiveness must come as a result of the Father's future acceptance of Christ's merit. Christ's work, in a sense, waits for man's response to it (faith) in order to be completed. Although all are invited to ascend to forgiveness by their faith, not everyone is actually given this verdict of righteousness. The Gospel does not give it, in this logic. Faith must go to the forgiving judgment seat, rising above God's ubiquitous wrath on earth, transporting the believer to where justification happens in heaven. This either/or scheme leaves no tension between the law, God's wrath, and the Gospel, God's justification. They never have to be coordinated, because they are never together. The Gospel verdict is placed in heaven safe from unbelievers and rejection.

The proponent of objective justification "seems to hate so much" the "throne of grace" language, because it is just a picture, not the full, biblical presentation of the matter.[33] "Faith neither merits, nor makes preparation for salvation, but only receives it. Faith cannot properly be called a 'condition' of Salvation, because all conditions are fulfilled in Christ Jesus."[34] It is dishonest to use someone's own language and authority to say something they never defended or said—giving faith a more prominent role in grounding justification than Christ's resurrection. The "throne of grace" is a fine analogy, understood biblically, but no illustration can give an exhaustive biblical picture of justification. That analogy was never claimed to be the final word on justification for all time. When old Lutheran dogmaticians spoke in this way, they used this forensic idea of a courtroom before God to show that justification was not an infusing of righteousness, as Rome taught. They did not set up this analogy as the fundamental axiom of their theological system—they were far too respectful of the nuance of the scriptural picture. This analogy—really the rational assumptions concealed behind it—becomes the controlling paradigm, taking priority over what Scripture actually says.

In addition to the logical difficulties of a world justification in Christ, there is also the thought that God's forgiveness is unworthy of unbelievers who will reject it. This is a practical difficulty: the Gospel absolution

---

[33]Eric Stefanski, "Theses on the Article of Justification: A Refutation of the ACLC's Critique: Part 6."

[34]Martin Diers, "Objective Justification," 10.

can, and is often, abused. Removing the verdict of righteousness—true justification—from the Gospel itself, keeps unrighteous unbelievers from sullying Christ's pure forgiveness. Faith, in essence, transports believers to God's gracious verdict, leaving it inaccessible to anyone without faith. While presenting no opportunity for unbelievers to make Christ's justification look ineffective, it leaves no earthly avenue for faith and true repentance.

A simple state of affairs exists if faith makes forgiveness real: "A person is either appealing to the Law in unbelief or he is appealing in faith to the Throne of Grace for mercy. The former stands condemned before God, not justified; the latter stands justified before God, not condemned."[35] While true, from man's side, there is no real Gospel for the unbeliever who is always under God's wrath. Quoting Jn. 3:16–18, Rydecki says: "It really is just that simple."[36] This section of Scripture speaks of the final result for man—it does not define the Gospel for us. God's love is a motivating factor for Christ's atonement, but love is not justification. The Gospel, to bring to faith, must have and bestow forgiveness—an empty offer does *not* change man's heart. Without the tension of condemnation and perfected justification, the work of Christ has not yet had an effect for mankind. In other words, we must wait and have faith before the work of Christ is effective for mankind. Only when we convert the ineffective merit of Christ by faith, do we find Gospel—that is, God's actual forgiveness. We should pity the poor souls who are given this gospel.

An uncompleted, undeclared salvation is no salvation at all. One early denier of objective justification claims: "In the Gospel God shows the sinner a way out, which can redeem him from death and damnation and bring about the forgiveness of his sins."[37] Quoting 17th century words in order to avoid defining the effect of the Gospel, does no good for anyone.

"Objective Justification is the Father's declaration that He has accepted what Christ has done in the Atonement."[38] This completed aspect of forgiveness is what faith relies on, or else faith itself becomes

---

[35] Paul Rydecki, "The Forensic Appeal to the Throne of Grace," 13.
[36] Paul Rydecki, "The Forensic Appeal to the Throne of Grace," 19.
[37] G. Fritschel, quoted in: Walther, *Justification—Objective and Subjective*, 22.
[38] Martin Diers, "Objective Justification," 9.

the work that completes salvation. The "article of justification" includes "only the grace of God, the merit of Christ, and faith, which receives this in the promise of the Gospel, whereby the righteousness of Christ is imputed to us, whence we receive and have forgiveness of sins, reconciliation with God, sonship, and heirship of eternal life" (FC SD 3:25). These things exist objectively, and faith receives them. Faith does not create them. The absolution of Christ—and in Him, the world—speaks to the finality of the atonement and its acceptance by the Father.

The atonement, in abstract, without any recognition by the Father for man's sake, would not be a comfort or foothold for faith. If the Gospel is merely the winning, payment, or acquiring of righteousness, it still has nothing to do with people. Deniers of objective justification will talk much about the atonement, but forgiveness is not a present reality—it is faith that makes the Gospel come to life for them. This is exemplified in a summary of 2 Cor. 5:19: Paul "is simply expressing the thought by this that saving grace—the grace of eternal life, the grace of justification—is now acquired for the whole world."[39] Denials of objective justification use words expressing potential: "ELDoNA treats and speaks of the acquisition of the pronouncement as a potential pronouncement."[40] The Gospel—forgiveness—is missing, because justification is made impotent without the involvement of man. The Gospel, however, actually gives what it describes. "This righteousness is offered us by the Holy Ghost through the Gospel and in the Sacraments, and is applied, appropriated, and received through faith, whence believers have reconciliation with God, forgiveness of sins, the grace of God, sonship, and heirship of eternal life" (FC SD 3:16). The doctrine of objective justification brackets one side of justification in order to preserve the integrity and character of the Gospel itself.

This is the logical stumbling block: the forgiven world, from God's point of view, are not all individually forgiven, even for many who hear the Gospel.

> . . . we find the essence of objective justification reduced
> to a *logical* absurdity [by its deniers]; an absurdity simply
> because God's Word also tells me that I am never to bring
> the comfort of the *Gospel* to someone I know is willfully and

---

[39] George Fritschel (1909), quoted in: Rick Curia, *History of Objective or Universal Justification*, 66.

[40] ACLC, "Critique of ELDoNA," 28.

persistently impenitent. . . . *Does* his unbelief make that message [of the forgiveness] mere empty words; in actuality, then, make God into a liar?[41]

A modern denier of objective justification avers: "For, if justification is justification, if all sinners are indeed declared and accepted by God as righteous and holy (i.e., 'given the status of saints'), what further need is there for another justification?"[42] But not all justification in Scripture is justification by faith, just as "they *are* not all Israel who *are* of Israel" (Rom. 9:6; NKJV). This is not a matter of balancing two opposing objects, as in a zero-sum game, because there is no contradiction. Rather, there is the closest unity between these two universal verdicts. "The real problem for those who won't accept the truth of objective justification lies in the conflict of human reason when it has to deal with both Law and Gospel."[43]

This supposed new teaching is rather an increased emphasis on a denied aspect of Christ's Word: "The doctrine of Objective Justification, prior to the Absolution Controversy, was treated as a part of the Vicarious Atonement and Justification by Faith."[44] The absolution controversy of the 19th century was not about faith in the Gospel, which the Reformers expended much energy on, but the very essence of the Gospel. "The Augustanans [who denied objective justification] maintained that the Gospel imparts the forgiveness of sins to believers, but not to unbelievers." In practice, the Gospel does look ineffective: "How was the forgiveness of sins *powerfully imparted* to an unbeliever who nevertheless, remained unabsolved?" So "The Augustanans taught: The Gospel contains, holds forth, and offers the forgiveness of sins to all who hear it, but this forgiveness is given, imparted, and presented only to those who in faith receive it."[45] While this matches man's experience better, the Christian should be able to answer this question without referring to his participation in it: when is God satisfied and appeased over man's sin in totality?

---

[41] Rick Curia, *History of Objective or Universal Justification*, 31.

[42] Notice the Kokomo-style definition of objective justification. Vernon Harley, "Synergism—Its Logical Association with General Justification."

[43] Rick Curia, *History of Objective or Universal Justification*, 31.

[44] Martin Diers, "Objective Justification," 6.

[45] J. Magnus Rohne, *Norwegian Lutheranism up to 1872* (New York: Macmillan, 1926), quoted in: Rick Curia, *History of Objective or Universal Justification*, 20.

Faith grasps what is already present in Christ: the forgiveness of sins. "Implicit in the idea that something can be grasped is the idea that it exists beforehand to be grasped; it must exist as an objective reality."[46] In contrast to modern Protestantism, with its practically exclusive focus on the personal, subjective side of Christianity, it should be asked: Is "the value of faith defined by the intrinsic value of the object it grasps?"[47] Or is the reception, or acceptance, of Christ the real meat and sum of Christianity?

The most prevalent denial of justification is not regarding the merits of Christ in themselves, but their applicability—to whom do they apply and avail? Objective justification is a "facet of the general biblical doctrine of justification."[48] If there is no other aspect, faith makes the Gospel forgiving and effective. Then, the means of grace are not a real offer or giving of justification, but morph into a contractual offer: the Gospel "invites all men to obtain this justification," but does not actually give it.[49] The Gospel then becomes an if/then statement: If man believes, God will forgive when man meets this obligation of faith.

> According to [a worldly] dictionary, a promise is an assurance given by one person to another that the former will or will not perform a specified act. God's promise to the sinner in his Word is that He will justify and save the sinner if and when the latter accepts Christ as his Redeemer from sin.[50]

This "gospel" is really a sales offer with a catch, not the actual absolution of sin. It removes all power from the Gospel itself and turns man into the animator of forgiveness. Man's promises are fickle, fading, and always conditioned, while God's promises are, in Christ Jesus, "always Yes" (2 Cor. 1:19). The promise of forgiveness is as certain as God Himself. This forgiveness was declared and exists for all in God's Son.

If the word of reconciliation is only an offer with an unmet condition, it is not actually the forgiveness of sins, but " 'to believe' means to accept that which is already present."[51] "The faith of the sinner does not

---

[46] Jon Buchholz, "Jesus Canceled Your Debt!," 13

[47] Jon Buchholz, "Jesus Canceled Your Debt!," 17.

[48] Rick Curia, *History of Objective or Universal Justification*, 3.

[49] Maier, "A Summary Exposition of Justification," 30.

[50] Maier, "A Summary Exposition of Justification," 9.

[51] George Stoeckhardt, "[Yet a Word Concerning Justification]," quoted in: Rick Curia, *History of Objective or Universal Justification*, 55.

effect an additional change in the disposition of the reconciled God."[52] The verdict of righteousness, which arrives in the Gospel, is because of Christ's death and resurrection, not our acceptance of it. This is why any sinner can be forgiven—Christ was justified in our place on behalf of all mankind. He completed the transaction. His forgiveness is no less universal than the atonement. "Therefore we do not preach of and about forgiveness of sins, but we preach forgiveness itself; we offer to men a finished product, not a future possibility."[53] "Objective Justification is God's declaration that the Atonement which Jesus accomplished is, in fact, complete."[54]

The counterpart to Christ's death is His justification, when Christ's work and payment was accepted by the Father and declared as such. Consider the words of Joseph Augustus Seiss (1823–1904), a General Synod theologian (and not a Missouri Synod man in the least), who is known mostly for his peculiar and heretical millennialist views:

> A dead Christ, although having met the whole penalty due to our sins, is not all that is required. With nothing but His death upon the cross to rest on, however meritorious that death, we are still left without the satisfying demonstration that it has been accepted, that the debt has been paid, and that He is able to save unto the uttermost. Good Friday must have an Easter to follow it, as well as a Christmas to precede it. We need a living Saviour, a Master of death, one whom the Law having slain as a substitute for sinners could not hold under its power, and hence the glorious Resurrection of Christ as well as His sacrificial death. Otherwise, how could we be sure that His sacrifice of His life in our stead really has availed for our justification and release? Saving faith must accordingly take in the Saviour risen again from the dead, as well as His vicarious death. He was "delivered for our offenses," but had to be "raised again for our justification;" for so the Word is, "If Christ be not raised, your faith is vain; ye are yet in your sins."[55]

---

[52]Theodore Engelder, "Objective Justification," *CTM* IV (1933), quoted in: Rick Curia, *History of Objective or Universal Justification*, 34.

[53]Edward Koehler, "Objective Justification," *CTM* XVI (April 1945), quoted in: Rick Curia, *History of Objective or Universal Justification*, 95.

[54]Martin Diers, "Objective Justification," 14.

[55]Joseph A. Seiss, "Remarks on 'The Relation of Justification to the Doctrine of the Church'," *The Second General Conference of Lutherans in America, Philadelphia, April 1-3, 1902: Proceedings, Essays and Debates* (Newberry, SC: Lutheran Publication Board, 1904; http://play.google.com/books/reader?id=opQsAAAAYAAJ),

In the same response to a one-sided conference essay focusing solely on the death of Christ, Seiss directly ties justification to Christ's resurrection:

> . . . along with such an intense emphasizing of the death of Christ as the supreme thing embraced by faith, it might be well to note what rendered that death for our sins of such effective worth, and the demonstration of its acceptance furnished by our Savior's resurrection, as likewise entering very essentially into what faith embraces as the ground of our justification.[56]

Not only was the debt paid, it was imputed to Christ, and, in His justification, we are forgiven. As all died in His death, so, from the standpoint of God's reconciliation, we are all justified in Christ. We can say confidently, "God is no longer wrathful in Christ" to anyone, because God was reconciled to the world in His Son.

A Gospel energized by man's faith is not something an unbeliever can rely on. But, thankfully, the Gospel is a real, powerful absolution, as Luther taught us: "Even he who does not believe that he is free and his sins forgiven shall also learn, in due time, how assuredly his sins were forgiven, even though he did not believe it."[57] The Gospel is an active power—a true forgiving of sins—while at the same time the law condemns, binding sinners. Both are God's work. The Gospel is not an incomplete, ineffective batch of ingredients awaiting the missing ingredient of faith. This modern Gospel receptionism turns man and his response to the Gospel into the main power of Christianity, in place of Christ and His Gospel. A Christian should be able to state what Christ's death and resurrection mean for the one without faith.

78.

[56] Joseph Seiss, "Remarks on 'The Relation of Justification'," 79.
[57] "The Keys" (1530), LW 40:366–367.

Chapter 16

Gospel Factualism

Another danger, which has manifested itself more recently, is to present objective justification as a standalone doctrine. Without the safeguards of the subjective aspect and the "in Christ" qualifier, it leads to the conclusion that people can possess justification outside of Christ. To talk of forgiveness being imputed to individuals who do not believe, and are therefore outside of Christ, is incorrect. Objective justification expresses the impetus for the Gospel's forgiveness in time, but people are still under God's wrath until individually freed. No one person is freed from sin without knowledge of Christ and the forgiveness that comes in the Gospel.

When objective justification is applied to individuals who are outside of Christ, there is an implicit denial of the efficacy of the law. The objective aspect overwhelms and subsumes the subjective, making justification entirely a fact of the past. This changes how the Gospel is communicated. If forgiveness is completely relegated to the past, the Gospel is simply a reminder of what has already happened without the sinner's knowledge. Instead of preaching one into Christ by faith, it leads one to take this forgiveness for granted: "The idea, that every individual has already been justified and just need to be made aware of this, is not supported by the Bible or the Confessions."[1] "There is no such thing as 'universal individual justification.'"[2]

---

[1] Magnus Sørensen, "The Justification of Christ," 35.
[2] Jon Buchholz, "Jesus Canceled Your Debt!," 12.

If objective justification happened in the past for every individual, so that the need for personal repentance and faith is minimized, then "absolution does not effect forgiveness but only inform[s] about an already established fact."[3] Yet something *does* happen for the individual in faith, but not in regards to the reality of forgiveness. Man's state does change—from condemnation to one of grace, free of God's wrath. If nothing changed for man in the spoken absolution, "Such a position would deny the power of absolution as much as the complete denial of universal justification that the early Synodical Conference adopted the terminology to reject."[4]

The duality of the two verdicts must be upheld, because "God in Christ sees the world as righteous, but in Adam, outside Christ, the world still stands condemned (John 3:36)."[5] Christians, who still have the old Adam as long as they are in this world, do not move beyond the power of the law. "It must be proclaimed in the church and to the world that God is reconciled and at peace with all (Gospel), just as that God is angry and punishes sinners (law) must be proclaimed in the church and to the world."[6]

Forgiveness, the justification of all mankind, is only in Christ, so it must be distributed. Faith does not rely on an unreachable absolution, but the personal application of the objective justification that comes in the Gospel. "Unfortunately some of the infelicitous expressions found in our circles in defense of universal justification might sound remarkably like Samuel Huber."[7]

Preaching and the means of grace actually release from the bondage of sin—they do not merely inform of a change in status one was unaware of. As the Small Catechism tells us: Baptism "works forgiveness of sins, rescues from death and the devil, and gives eternal salvation to all who believe this." This is a divine activity of the Spirit, not just a pointer back to what has already been completed from man's point of view. If there is no change in the person's status before God, there is no justification as a result of the Gospel.

---

[3] Magnus Sørensen, "The Justification of Christ," 36.

[4] Thesis 45, Magnus N. Sørensen, "Theses on Universal Objective Justification," 2018 Convocation of the Orthodox Lutheran Confessional Conference.

[5] Thesis 77, Magnus Sørensen, "Theses on Universal Objective Justification."

[6] CTCR, "Theses on Justification," 20.

[7] Jon Buchholz, "Jesus Canceled Your Debt!," 24.

The grave danger in objective justification is to remove forgiveness from Christ. The dulling of the power of the Gospel is a practical error: "do we anesthetize our consciences by repeating the mantra 'God has already forgiven the whole world, and I am certainly included in that'?"[8] In contrast, faith is a living thing, feeding on Christ's life (Jn. 6:25–69).

Something actually happens when the Gospel imparts forgiveness and also when we receive it in faith. If the Gospel is just a reminder of what has already been done, the nature of the Christian message is altered. This short-circuits justification, because the universal absolution in Christ must be revealed to individuals—they must be actually forgiven in time and brought into Christ. This is either done or not done for the individual; it is not a universal act. This subjective aspect, which happens in time, is just as real as the objective aspect. This is a clear teaching of Scripture: "For sin will have no dominion over you, since you are not under law but under grace" (Rom. 6:14). Faith is not to be taken for granted, as it is when the objective verdict overwhelms the reality of subjective faith.

Objective justification does not negate God's wrath: "Whoever believes in the Son has eternal life; whoever does not obey the Son shall not see life, but the wrath of God remains on him" (Jn. 3:36). The law, which is a universal verdict in Adam, is still valid, insofar as we are outside of Christ. They are misled who "imagine that they have justifying faith, when in fact they continue to live impenitently in mortal sin and have no intention to amend their lives."[9] Yes, the world has forgiveness, but that justification is found solely in Christ. Outside of Christ there is only wrath. The call to repentance and the binding key require that sins not be forgiven. Those who remain captivated by sin and its power are not forgiven, even if they have the "fact" of objective justification.

As truly as all sin is absolved in the Gospel, so the law must truly condemn every sin: "it is also necessary and Scriptural, according to the terms of God's law, to speak of impenitent sinners as not justified and forgiven, but condemned."[10] The law is not a scarecrow to ignore once we learn of God's reconciliation in Christ: "The tension between

---

[8]Kurt Marquart, "Objective Justification," *Marquart's Works*, 6:81.

[9]CTCR, "Theses on Justification," 14.

[10]CTCR, "Theses on Justification," 15.

law and gospel [is] not just . . . a pedagogical device."[11] If this is not a widespread technical error, it is a practical error in many pulpits. It is easy to dance around the verdict of the law with Christian verbiage, without actually condemning sins and sinners. Conversely, when this is the case, the pardon of sins is assumed, since there is no exposed guilt to forgive. Both the law and the Gospel are to be fully used as divine powers. "Jesus did not say 'tell all people that they are already forgiven,' but 'If you forgive the sins of any, they are forgiven them.'"[12]

Both the effacing of objective justification and the false logic of applying objective justification to an individual outside of Christ are a "denial of the co-existence of Law and Gospel."[13] These errors are basically the same—they assume the law and the Gospel oppose and cancel one another. The verdicts in Adam and Christ are played against each other, instead of upheld as universally and objectively valid. Luther speaks of the reality outside of Christ:

> God assures us: "Sin, hell, judgment, and God's wrath have all been terminated by the Son." . . . Now what is still lacking? Why the judgment if all sin has been removed by the Son? The answer is that the judgment is incurred by man's refusal to accept Christ, the Son of God. Of course, man's sin, both that inherited from Adam and that committed by man himself, is deserving of death. But this judgment results from man's unwillingness to hear, to tolerate, and to accept the Savior, who removed sin, bore it on His shoulders, and locked up the portals of hell.[14]

Both errors uplift one particular divine judgment above the other. Although it may be said that only unbelief condemns, because all sins are forgiven in Christ, that is true only from God's view in Christ, where there is no sin. Apart from faith (which implies Christ), man is under the law, which condemns his real sins and justly damns, but a denier of objective justification falsely suggests: "Why put justified, forgiven sinners in jeopardy of being damned by giving them an opportunity to reject the Gospel, especially if, as some are now saying, 'only refusal to believe damns'?"[15] Since man is born into Adam, all are born into

---

[11] Magnus Sørensen, "The Justification of Christ," 17.

[12] Magnus Sørensen, "The Justification of Christ," 34.

[13] Tom Hardt, "Justification and Easter," 59.

[14] Sermon on Jn. 3:19 (Sept. 21, 1538), LW 22:382.

[15] Vernon Harley, "Synergism—Its Logical Association with General Justification."

God's wrath and condemnation. Forgiveness is not an automatic fact to be taken for granted, but a powerful, imparting promise. Both keys, the twin powers of binding and loosing sin, are divine and effective.

It is astutely asked: "Does Objective Justification imply that the only real sin is unbelief, or does it confess that those who are damned bear the full guilt of their sin?"[16] In other words, are actual sins to be condemned, or are all sins forgiven to fleshly man, so that unbelief is the only issue God could possibly have with him? The answer is that both are correct. It is true, from God's side, since there is no sin unforgiven in Christ, who is received only in faith. But the subjective aspect of the law is truly real—it condemns all sins, which anger God outside of Christ. "Where the guilt of sin remains, God is still one's enemy."[17]

The Spirit will convict "concerning sin, because they do not believe in me" (Jn. 16:9). Unbelief means that one is entirely in Adam, under the curse. Christ's justification did not dull the effect and power of the law. The law does not just convict of unbelief (which is a root sin), but it exposes the lack of love displayed in every respect before the righteous God. "Speaking according to the acquisition of salvation, He is wroth [has wrath] with no man any longer, but speaking according to the appropriation, He is wroth [wrathful] with everyone who is not in Christ."[18] If either verdict is lost, the Gospel ceases to be a present comfort and sustainer of divine faith.

If God is merely angry at humanity and not reconciled, there is no Gospel. If there is no wrath in the law subjectively applied to individuals as sinners, there is no corresponding need for comfort. Salvation is not an idea or intellectual curiosity to ponder; God's still burning wrath makes redemption the greatest need. If we follow the scriptural pattern, this mystery will not be resolved, despite how intensely human reason desires it. It was asked of Walther: how does "the Gospel as an absolution of the whole world of sinners, harmonize with those Scripture passages which speak of God's wrath upon the world lying in wickedness, in particular upon the unbelievers. Walther answers by means of the distinction between Law and Gospel."[19] Both universal judgments are to be applied.

---

[16]Martin Diers, "Objective Justification," 6.

[17]Martin Diers, "Objective Justification," 7.

[18]Walther, *Justification—Objective and Subjective*, 10.

[19]F. Pieper, "Walther as Theologian: Justification, Universal," 5.

We reconcile men by the Gospel, but we do not reconcile difficulties in the Word of God by pitting its teachings against each other.

The drive to unify the twin judgments of God changes the Gospel from a true means of justification into something less. Objective justification may become a caricature, just a post-it note marking what happened far away from the present. This may raise self-awareness, but it is not a truly powerful release from sin and God's wrath.

> Is [the Gospel], too, a *setting free*, or merely a *proclamation* of the setting free that has already occurred? *Answer:* . . . precisely through the Gospel occurs the conveying of what is in God's heart . . . a proclamation that really brings and gives the forgiveness. . . . *The absolution in the Gospel is nothing else than a repetition of the factual absolution which has already happened through the resurrection of Jesus Christ from the dead.*[20]

The Gospel offers and bestows a true release from guilt, so that it personally applies what is in Christ. The Gospel is not just evidentiary, witnessing to the past, but a living proclamation that creates faith. So, also, the law's verdict is unabated by justification in Christ. "For the wrath of God is revealed from heaven against all ungodliness and unrighteousness of men, who suppress the truth in unrighteousness" (Rom. 1:18).

The law and the Gospel are true judicial acts. Something objectively happens in both, revealing man's state before God. Neither objective justification, nor subjective justification conflict, making the other unnecessary—both emphases hold true in correct biblical teaching. We may talk about one or the other separately, at different times, but we may not ever completely separate them.

While it is tempting to get wrapped up in debates of the most precise terms and phrases, Christ's resurrection is meant to be used to free sinners. The Word of Christ delivers resurrection life to us, just as much as the law condemns to hell. We must have more than just talk about forgiveness and condemnation, but also a real use of the keys, so these heavenly powers are exercised among us. We may not change God's Word to fit our preconceived notions or what fleshly man desires to hear.

---

[20]Convention of the Missouri Synod (1860), trans. and quoted in: Tom Hardt, "Justification and Easter," 64.

Chapter 17

The Cause of our Absolution

In modern Protestantism the death of Christ is preeminent and over-shadows His resurrection. Theologically, His rising from the dead plays little to no role, but, in the Bible, the resurrection of our Lord is not an add-on, but the highly significant and necessary completion of Christ's redemptive work. It is the cause and source of our redemption, just as much as Adam is the origin of man's sin: "So then as through one trespass [Adam's sin] there resulted condemnation for all men, even so through one act of righteousness there resulted justification of life to all men" (Rom. 5:18; Amplified Bible). "Only a Calvinistic exegesis could explain this passage to the effect that only the elect are justified."[1]

Since the world was absolved in Christ, the Word is not merely a reminder of, or new information about, an old fact. Forgiveness derives its power from Christ's work. The Gospel, in any form, is a pardon or absolution in itself. It brings forgiveness, which justifies individuals. It is the complement to Christ's death: "As we were co-punished in Christ's death, we are again co-absolved from our sins in his resurrection."[2]

The modern justification debate is not over the atonement, but the

---

[1] Walther, quoted in: F. Pieper, "Walther as Theologian: Justification, Universal," 4.

[2] Convention of the Missouri Synod (1860), quoted in: Tom Hardt, "Justification and Easter," 61.

effect of it. Those who deny objective justification also deny that the absolution of Christ results in justification for mankind, leaving no forgiveness in the Gospel for all men. Despite this, Christ's resurrection, the taking away of our sin, is "a substitution of no less importance than that of His death."[3] This resurrection is the bookend to Christ's negative punishment. Scripture expressly states that a dead Christ would allow for no forgiveness and no comfort: "if Christ is not risen, your faith *is* futile; you are still in your sins!" (1 Cor. 15:17; NKJV). The means of grace effectively distribute to individuals the content and results of Easter. This Word of Christ is the connection between Christ and individuals.

The forgiveness present in the Gospel should "not [be] seen as a justification that stands far off in the distance," which requires some work of man to bring near. It is delivered by the Word of the Gospel, which creates faith. It informs of what Christ has already done, but also much more. "It is, rather, such an announcement which gives what it announces at the same time it announces it."[4] A real absolution must reach men condemned in Adam. It must be heard, as forgiveness must be applied to real sins. The true doctrine of God's new relationship to man in Christ (objective justification) does not help any individual, unless he has personally heard and believed. "The power of reconciliation, namely, the forgiveness of sins for all men, is brought by means of the Gospel to all who hear it." Christ's work must be effective for all, if the results are presently available for all. The Lutheran position of a completed general justification has been emphasized against "the general reformed-enthusiast view that God's Word is only a powerless announcement, which actually only first acquires a powerful content, through faith or something else in those who hear it."[5]

The resurrection of Christ "was equally as substitutionary as His passion."[6] No Lutheran disputes that the death of Jesus was valid for all people, rather, the dispute is over the consequence of His resurrection,

---

[3] Tom Hardt, "Justification and Easter," 61.

[4] Theodore Julius Brohm (1808–1881), "[Paper Concerning the Intimate Connection of the Doctrine of Absolution with that of Justification]," quoted in: Rick Curia, *History of Objective or Universal Justification*, 16, 17.

[5] Rick Curia, *History of Objective or Universal Justification*, 19.

[6] John Schaller, quoted in: Rick Curia, *History of Objective or Universal Justification*, 69.

which was His absolution. The Lord Jesus "was delivered up for our trespasses and raised for our justification" (Rom. 4:25). "Now if Christ was raised again for the sake of our (as it says according to the original text) justification, then precisely the resurrection must be the ground on which it rests, without which it would be impossible."[7] It was not Christ who needed personal absolution, but His resurrection was the absolution of the sins of the world, which rested on Him. A Christian does not believe that when the sinner is absolved, Christ is absolved in every earthly absolution. Christ, in His resurrection, was absolved substitutionally, or vicariously, on behalf of all.

Despite the express link in Rom. 4:25 between Christ's rising and justification, other scriptural statements mentioning faith are used against it: "Paul, when he expressly discusses justification in Romans 3 and 4, does not know of a justification apart from faith."[8] Rationalist assumptions rule out what Paul actually says. In contrast, one translation reads: "[Christ] was raised to life because of the acquittal secured for us" (Rom. 4:25; Weymouth New Testament). Justification is always a verdict, a real divine act.

Those who leave out the objective dimension of forgiveness worry it will lead to carnal security, so that unbelievers will take this precious freedom for granted, be emboldened, and trample it. This will always be a danger and real occurrence. "For you were called to freedom, brothers. Only do not use your freedom as an opportunity for the flesh, but through love serve one another" (Gal. 5:13). The freedom of the Gospel will be abused by those who remain in slavery to sin. They are truly absolved by the Word, but have no part in Christ. They must also be condemned—not in a general and abstract way, but personally.

"The fear that people may abuse this doctrine [of objective justification] dare not restrain the truth. And this is just what keeps back the fanatics from proclaiming it without restriction. They imagine that it leads to carnal security."[9] The solution for those who do not want the absolution abused is to remove Christ's forgiveness from the Gospel. Forgiveness cannot be rejected if it is not identified with the Gospel.

---

[7] Walther, *Justification—Objective and Subjective*, 18.

[8] ELDoNA, "Theses on the Article of Justification," 5.

[9] Discussion of theses accepted at the first convention of the Synodical Conference (1872), quoted in: Rick Curia, *History of Objective or Universal Justification*, 38.

It leads to what is stated in this caricature: "God informs us of the reconciliation effected by Christ through the Gospel and at the same time tells us what conditions we must fulfill that He now may *actually* forgive and justify us: we must, namely, first believe."[10] Or, in the words of one who actually denied the power of God's absolution: "According to the teaching of the Bible, neither the forgiveness of sins nor the righteousness which is valid before God can be spoken to a man until he believes in Christ. . . . "[11]

Luther taught that the Gospel and the law, the keys of the kingdom, do not depend on man's belief:

> We are not talking here either about people's belief or disbelief regarding the efficacy of the keys. We realize that few believe. We are speaking of what the keys accomplish and give. He who does not accept what the keys give receives, of course, nothing. But this is not the key's fault. Many do not believe the gospel, but this does not mean that the gospel is not true or effective. A king gives you a castle. If you do not accept it, then it is not the king's fault, nor is he guilty of a lie. But you have deceived yourself and the fault is yours. The king certainly gave it.[12]

Luther explains the import of objective justification, that forgiveness is not somewhere outside the Gospel, but that it is explicitly here for all the world because the Father "has already declared the whole world to be righteous in Christ."[13] This is the strongest Gospel statement: justification is complete in Christ and applies universally. This living power allows the Gospel to be spoken to all individuals, so that sins are forgiven, before man believes or rejects. This present reality of forgiveness is indeed what is believed or rejected, what is true in Christ and has been previously declared in Him.

The modern deniers of objective justification "deny the fullness, the freedom and the completeness of the gospel. They are unwilling to say in an unqualified and unconditional way, 'God has forgiven your

---

[10]Carl Zorn, quoted in: Rick Curia, *History of Objective or Universal Justification*, 58.

[11]Henry August Allwardt, "Missouri's Further Apostasy from the Doctrine of the Lutheran Church" (1889), quoted in: Rick Curia, *History of Objective or Universal Justification*, 53.

[12]"The Keys" (1530), LW 40:367.

[13]*Brief Statement of the Missouri Synod*, 6.

sins in Christ! God canceled your debt in Christ!' "[14] This absolution for the world is a tangible reality actually given to sinners, not an absent abstraction from which to make logical deductions. It directly determines and effects the concrete nature of preaching. To acknowledge the reality of objective justification is to believe that "reconciliation with God, righteousness, entitlement to be children of God, . . . lies there in readiness and is distributed in the holy Christian church through the Gospel."[15] If the Church does not have the power to forgive sins, it has nothing of substance to offer men. To preach Christ, in this case, would be merely to preach possibilities. Preaching into faith does not mean ignoring Christ any more than preaching Christ crucified means preaching a dead Christ who cannot forgive. The promise "creates faith, so that justification is received *per fidem* [through faith] as a gift of God."[16] Justification, complete in itself, comes in the promise, because the promise is a real absolution from God. There is the closest relationship between justification by faith and the cause of absolution in general—they are one in Christ.

Walther calls objective justification the "doctrine of the perfection of the redemption of Christ."[17] From God's side, it is finished; Christ is risen to die no more. But we dare not use man's reception of the Gospel against the forgiving Word itself. The logic goes: because not all believe, there is no salvation—something must be missing from the Gospel itself. Salvation is essentially the forgiveness of sins, relayed to those in Adam. Luther explains this connection in his Small Catechism: "For where there is forgiveness of sins, there is also life and salvation."

The overemphasis on faith—the salvific objectification of faith—makes man the actor and cause of salvation, so that God is the problem to be solved and man is the solution. This is nothing but warmed-over law, no matter how many times the word "Gospel" or "faith" is spoken. Christ is of no effect, essentially, and is effectively dead to the unbeliever until man in his faith makes Him forgiving. "In contrast, the Scriptural teaching of objective justification says: God is no longer the Enemy,

---

[14] Jon Buchholz, "Jesus Canceled Your Debt!," 30.

[15] Walther, *Justification—Objective and Subjective*, 12.

[16] Martim Warth, "Justification through Faith in Article Four of the Apology," 107.

[17] Walther, *Justification—Objective and Subjective*, 13.

Who is to be reconciled—but man is that."[18] The emphasis of objective justification is on what is real before faith, defining the effectiveness of the Gospel itself. 2 Cor. 5:19 declares "that the relationship between two parties has *fundamentally changed*. God changes His relationship to the world."[19] The Gospel does not first require a change of attitude in man or imply that individuals have already modified their relationship to God. Both errors neuter the power of the Gospel key. Justification happened in Christ, from whom all forgiveness begins and flows in the Gospel we hear and handle. This the contact point, without which men, in particular, receive no forgiveness. This communication of forgiveness is the reason why the teaching of objective justification is so necessary.

Objective justification tells us that the Gospel can be applied to all people without discrimination. "It therefore is not true that God has let us be reconciled through Christ in order that He 'might be able' to forgive our sins and to justify us, but rather that the reconciliation through Christ is our justification and the forgiveness of sins, and of those of the whole world."[20] That truth must not be used against the law; sin must also be condemned with God's living wrath. The law indirectly serves the Gospel by pointing out and exposing sin, making sin actually sinful. "Yet if it had not been for the law, I would not have known sin" (Rom. 7:7). It is not necessary to use objective justification terminology or to express the Gospel in such words, but it is implicit and a part of the inspired doctrine. Neither is it required to talk about faith to forgive sins—to give the full absolution of God. Both aspects are true, but in the face of the denial of the perfect reconciliation of God accomplished by Christ, it has become more necessary than ever to defend the truth of the origin and effectiveness of forgiveness.

In the "personal justification of the individual," the believer "seizes through faith the universal justification which is present before all faith."[21] If the believer, with his faith, is not made alive to grasp the forgiveness actually present in the Gospel, what actually makes him

---

[18] Walther, *Justification—Objective and Subjective*, 14.

[19] John Schaller (1910), quoted in: Rick Curia, *History of Objective or Universal Justification*, 67.

[20] Carl Zorn, quoted in: Rick Curia, *History of Objective or Universal Justification*, 59.

[21] August Pieper (1906), quoted in: Rick Curia, *History of Objective or Universal Justification*, 64.

renewed? Thankfully, the righteousness procured by faith remains a fixed reality, anchored in Christ, outside the individual, so he can be "absolutely certain of his justification."[22] Christ is not dead, but raised, and so "forgiveness is not just an unfulfilled promise that is available. It is a completed reality."[23]

---

[22] George Stoeckhardt, *Commentary of Paul's Letter to the Romans* (1907), quoted in: Rick Curia, *History of Objective or Universal Justification*, 65.

[23] Jon Buchholz, "Jesus Canceled Your Debt!," 13.

Chapter 18

Justified for the Sake of Faith, not Christ

Objective justification describes forgiveness from God's side, not man's. Though, if justification is only tied to faith, there is no other aspect, rendering it incomplete without man's involvement. The objective dimension of justification preserves the reality of forgiveness, which exists and has been declared in Christ. Christ's forgiveness is not completed by man's acceptance of it. Faith alone, to the Reformers, was simply the biblical way to express that "men cannot be justified before God by their own strength, merits, or works, . . . or satisfactions" (AC 4). But today, faith is what makes forgiveness real for many Protestants, so that "faith itself becomes with them a meritorious human work."[1]

As important and scriptural as true faith is, it does not justify as a cause and source of forgiveness in itself: "it is not faith which gives man value before God, but Christ, Whom faith embraces." Justification by faith is a simplistic slogan. "The expression, 'we become righteous through faith,' is a metonymy; that is, the container is here named in place of the content."[2] The traditional Lutheran phrasing is shorthand, but what was formerly assumed no longer can be, due to new errors.

The phrase "justified by faith alone" is, at best, incomplete. It can be defined to not require the death of Christ, let alone His resurrection.

---

[1]Walther, *Justification—Objective and Subjective*, 17.
[2]Walther, *Justification—Objective and Subjective*, 39.

The deniers of objective justification use a slogan as ultimate truth. In doing so they weaponize it instead of using it as an opening to magnify the glorious Gospel of Christ. Faith alone is an important emphasis, but it is not the full biblical picture: "You see that a person is justified by works and not by faith alone" (Jam. 2:24). This does not contradict Paul in Romans and Galatians: If something is called "faith" in a person ruled by sin, so that there are no good works and thus no Holy Spirit, there is no true faith. This so-called "faith" damns. We must seek the meaning and import the blessed Reformers intended by this slogan, not use it as a tool to cut off biblical understanding.

True Lutherans are not verbal legalists, since the Scriptures use many pictures and phrases to explain salvation. The truth is bigger than our limited summaries of it. In fact, the word "justify" need not always be articulated, any more than the word "faith" is needed to actually bestow justification and faith in Christ. "We do not say that one by necessity always has to use the expression: 'the world is justified in Christ' . . . for we know very well that this article of faith can be explained and represented completely and correctly by other words."[3] However, if one phrase is the only way to describe the matter, it has replaced the timeless Scripture that claims divine inspiration.

The main error defenders of the Gospel have fought for the better part of two centuries is the thought that conversion completes redemption. "The fanatics usually think of the matter [of salvation] as though Christ has brought to pass that which the Scripture calls atonement, so that God can now receive a man into heaven merely for the sake of his conversion."[4] This describes the general Protestant error today—the most dangerous and pressing one of our time. If there is nothing except the personal—so the basis of Christ's salvation is simply Christ's death—that leaves a theological gap that "faith" must fill. However, "Faith is passive in justification. It never enters the picture as a cause of justification, but always as an instrument of receiving the universal justification of God pronounced in the Gospel."[5] Faith, if it "does not merely grasp the righteousness already gained and bestowed," then

---

[3] 1871 German article Walther reprinted in *Lehre and Wehre*, quoted in: Tom Hardt, "Justification and Easter," 65.

[4] F. Pieper, "Walther as Theologian: Justification, Universal," 2.

[5] Wendland, quoted in: Jon Buchholz, "Jesus Canceled Your Debt!," 19.

"obtains a deserving character as a work of a good nature."[6] Faith, as the immediate and effective cause of justification, must fill the missing gap if Christ Himself did not do it in His rising. If there is no true justification completed before faith, then this increased role for faith is necessary. Despite how well it is spoken of and venerated, it has become a cursed work of the law.

Recent deniers of objective justification have made a very strange claim. They say that a prominent 20th century LCMS theologian, Robert Preus, who did significant work defending objective justification, changed his mind on this very teaching right before his death. While it would not damage the scriptural truth or undermine his previous arguments even if it were true, the faulty reasoning behind this conclusion is quite revealing. It is claimed that "Preus corrects himself in his *Justification and Rome*" and that Dr. Preus "retracted" his position on objective justification.[7] ELDoNA parrots this idea: "We note that the Rev. Dr. Robert Preus also came to this conclusion [that Objective Justification is a 'gross overstatement'] late in his life."[8] Their reasoning is much more instructive than their biased claim. Preus authored a book against the Roman church's errors on justification, but objective justification has not been historically denied by Rome—some of its theologians even have promoted it.[9]

The reason why they claim Robert Preus changed his position is because he could talk about the subjective aspect of justification fully and completely, without explicit reference to the objective aspect. ELDoNA quotes this statement from the 1997 posthumously published work *Justification and Rome*: "God just the same does not justify us prior to our faith. Nor do we become God's children in Christ in such a way that justification in the mind of God takes place before we believe." They then add another quote from the same work: "When does the imputation of Christ's righteousness take place? It did not take place when Christ, by doing and suffering, finished the work of atonement and reconciled the world to God. Then and there, when the sins of the world were imputed to Him and He took them, Christ became our righteousness and procured for us remission of sin, justification, and

---

[6]H.A. Preus, quoted in: Martin Diers, "Objective Justification," 3.

[7]Gregory Jackson, *Luther versus the Pietists*, 29, 126.

[8]ELDoNA, "Theses on the Article of Justification," 5–6.

[9]See the Hans Kueng quotes on pages 11 and 157.

eternal life."[10] The problem is, as Preus explained in 1960[11] and in 1982 (in the midst of the objective justification controversy in the LCMS), that the word "imputation" deals with subjective justification, not the objective element. Imputation deals only with the individual's state here, since for Preus, it means forgiveness is "secured (had)," which is "always *per fidem* [through faith]."[12] Traditionally, Lutherans used "imputation" only for personal justification by faith, since it means "to attribute, to ascribe, to transfer, confer, devolve [delegate] upon another the effect of a voluntary act by one's own estimate and decision."[13] In regards to the reception, and the clear subjective context of Preus' words, this is true. What the deniers cannot see is that the dual aspects of justification can be explained individually without contradiction, or even reference to each other.

The supposed contradiction between objective and subjective justification exists solely in man's imagination: "If all men were justified, i.e., declared righteous, absolved at the resurrection of Christ, but if men must be justified again (subjectively) by faith in order to be finally saved from the wrath of God, then quite obviously God wasn't at all serious in objective justification."[14] By placing the two verdicts in opposition, faith is disconnected from its object, Christ. This reasoning plays forgiveness in Christ against forgiveness received from Christ by faith, because "there are not two justifications (one general, universal and objective, the other subjective in the heart of man), but only one."[15] This is a common theme in the arguments against objective justification, while the proponents of objective justification see no diminishing of faith when talking of God's complete reconciliation. But a denier of objective justification can say that the

> teaching concerning an 'objective justification' and a 'subjective justification,' leads to the conclusion that there are two different acts or pronouncements of justification on God's part: one pronouncement made at the time of the death

---

[10]ELDoNA, "Theses on the Article of Justification," 6.

[11]Magnus Sørensen, "The Justification of Christ," 10.

[12]Robert Preus, "Justification as Taught by Post-Reformation Lutheran Theologians," 2.

[13]David Hollaz (1648–1713), quoted in: Heinrich Schmid, *The Doctrinal Theology of the Evangelical Lutheran Church*, 433.

[14]Vernon Harley, "Synergism—Its Logical Association with General Justification."

[15]Vernon Harley, "Synergism—Its Logical Association with General Justification."

and resurrection of Christ with regard to the whole world of unregenerate men (world or objective justification), but which saves none of them. . . . [16]

Forgiveness must come from somewhere—it is not created out of thin air by faith. Faith itself is created by this already existing forgiveness, which comes from our justification in Christ. The traditional faith versus works distinction is not able to fully delineate this new error regarding the role and place of faith in regards to Christ's merit; just because faith is divine and of the Spirit does not mean it, apart from Christ, causes God's anger to cease and makes Him reconciled toward man.

Instead of actually enlightening people with their supposed clarity of doctrine, deniers of objective justification nitpick various quotations and point out how in their own minds real Lutherans cannot logically be promoting objective justification:

> But Calov (mimicking Gerhard) makes a vital point here that demolishes the argument that all men have been justified in Christ. "For it says that Christ suffered and died both for our sake and in our place. However, He rose again, not in our place, but only for our sake." Since Calov and Gerhard expressly denied the fundamental tenet of "Objective Justification" that Christ was raised and justified in our place, it is either truly ignorant or truly disingenuous for its modern-day proponents to continue claiming validity for their novel doctrine in these Lutheran fathers.[17]

Calov, the same 17th century Lutheran, also wrote: "[Justification] is the *object* of faith in that it is offered by God in the Gospel; it is the *effect* [of faith] . . . in so far as grace having been apprehended by faith, the forgiveness of sins happens to us by that very act."[18] The first citation may be stating the obvious: Christ was not raised for us in the sense that we are not also raised, or that because Christ was personally justified, we need not be personally justified. It is a devilish error to say that, because we appropriate justification by faith, this excludes any prior source and basis for that righteousness.

---

[16] While it is true that some speak of two acts of justification, the verdict in Christ for mankind has not yet been received by all men. This happens only in the Gospel. Maier, "A Summary Exposition of Justification," 17.

[17] Eric Stefanski, "Theses on the Article of Justification: A Refutation of the ACLC's Critique: Part 5."

[18] Quoted in: Kurt Marquart, "Objective Justification," *Marquart's Works*, 6:72.

Deniers of objective justification do not just accuse orthodox Lutheran theologians of the 20th and 17th centuries of sloppiness; they go after the original Lutheran, Luther, who taught quite forcefully the completed aspect of redemption. In their official theses, ELDoNA implicitly accuses Luther of being so shoddy a theologian that he had to "correct" himself within a single work. While early Luther is often played against mature Luther by theological liberals, here the Luther six pages more mature has to correct the Luther six pages younger: "Luther's correction on p. 286 of his 1535 lectures on Galatians (AE, vol. 26) to what he said on p. 280 . . . is wrongly used by some to accuse him of teaching what he did not teach regarding Justification."[19] This shows how little they understand and respect the teaching of Luther.

Martin Luther did not have to reconcile scriptural teachings in each page, sentence, or work; he let them stand complete, just as they are established in Scripture. Justification by faith is not a "correction" to the fact that sin is demolished as the result of Christ's work for all the world—that in Christ "the whole world is purged and expiated from all sins." These are merely different aspects of forgiveness, one from the angle of Christ's effective work and the other from man's ownership of it. Luther spoke of the objective aspect as definitively as any modern proponent of objective justification:

> And this is our highest comfort, to clothe and wrap Christ this way in my sins, your sins, and the sins of the entire world, and in this behold Him bearing all sin. . . . if He is truly the Lamb of God who takes away the sins of the world, who became a curse for us, and who was wrapped in our sins, it necessarily follows that we cannot be justified and take away sins through love. For God has laid our sins, not upon us but upon Christ, His Son. If they are taken away by Him, then they cannot be taken away by us. . . . When the merciful Father saw that we were being oppressed through the Law, that we were being held under a curse, and that we could not be liberated from it by another, He sent His Son into the world, heaped all the sins of all men upon Him, and said to Him: "Be Peter the denier; Paul the persecutor, blasphemer, and assaulter; David the adulterer; the sinner who ate the apple in Paradise; the thief on the cross. In short, be the person of all men, the one who has committed the sins of all men. And see to it that you pay and make satisfaction for them." Now the Law comes and says: "I find

---

[19]ELDoNA, "Theses on the Article of Justification," 8.

Him a sinner, who takes upon Himself the sins of all men. I do not see any other sins than those in Him. Therefore let Him die on the cross!" And so it attacks Him and kills Him. By this deed the whole world is purged and expiated from all sins, and thus, set free from death and from every evil. But when sin and death have been abolished by this one man, God does not want to see anything else in the whole world, especially if it were to believe, except sheer cleansing and righteousness. And if any remnants of sins are to remain, still for the sake of Christ, the shining Sun, God would not notice them.[20]

Sin is no more in Christ—it is dead and powerless from God's point of view. "So the fact that the wrath of God is a completely extant and a totally and continuingly operative factor in God's relationship" to unbelieving man, does not negate the absolution of mankind in Christ—that which the Gospel actually declares before faith can occur.[21] Man does not enjoy and receive this benefit personally until faith is given, but it is objectively true that, in Christ, God sees no sin on the world at all—it has all died in Jesus. The resurrection of our Lord is the final nail in the coffin of sin, so that God is "not counting their trespasses against" mankind. To make God simply wrathful at the world requires reducing the content of reconciliation, so that wrath is still the dominating relationship of God to the world.

"Propitiate" or "appease" or "placate" or "reconcile", thus conceived [apart from any objective justification], would then mean temporarily to allay, mitigate, or reduce the intensity of the divine wrath against the world of sinners, to restrain its full "flashing forth" against the unregenerate (as this will occur on judgment day and through eternity).[22]

A non-objective justification—one for which Christ died to possibly make real one day—would make sin more real than grace, leaving nothing for weak sinners to rely on but their own ability to grasp righteousness from the heavenly places. However, our righteousness is complete in the risen Christ, due to His work on our behalf: "And you, who were dead in your trespasses and the uncircumcision of your flesh, God made alive together with him, having forgiven us all our trespasses, by canceling the record of debt that stood against us with its legal demands. This

---

[20]"Lectures on Galatians" (1535), LW 26:279–80.

[21]Maier, "A Summary Exposition of Justification," 17.

[22]Maier, "A Summary Exposition of Justification," 34.

he set aside, nailing it to the cross" (Col. 2:13–14).

Older Lutherans were not slogan theologians, repeating mantras to avoid careful distinctions.

> It is one thing to be justified on account of faith and another to be justified by faith. In the former view, faith is the meritorious, in the latter, the instrumental cause. (There must be an organ by which I come into the possession and enjoyment of what someone offers me.) We are not justified on account of faith as a merit, but by faith which lays hold of the merit of Christ.[23]

Faith saves because it receives Christ, not because it takes the place of Christ and His resurrection. We may not say that the faith of the believer effectively raises Christ, bringing absolution and righteousness forth from the Father and changing God's relationship to man. That would make faith a propitiatory sacrifice—the new mass, in confessional terms—not merely a gift of God, but something that reconciles or makes God redemptive. Man's attitude towards God becomes salvific, in a sacrificial way.

> The fanatics . . . do not believe that through Christ everything without exception has happened which had to happen in order for God to be able to save us and give us eternal life. . . . Something, they think, still remains for man to do, and this something, they think, is conversion.[24]

Those who deny objective justification, the completeness of justification from God's viewpoint,

> teach that in justification the human attitude is a condition, in view of which God forgives men their sins . . . [so that the] Ohio [synod] must not issue as it watchword, 'justification *through* the act of faith,' but 'justification and forgiveness on account of the act of faith, on account of the right attitude.' Ohio has logically destroyed the Lutheran doctrine of justification through faith and joined the camp of the papists.[25]

---

[23] Johann Gerhard, quoted in: C.F.W. Walther, *The Proper Distinction between Law and Gospel,* trans. W.H.T. Dau (St. Louis: Concordia Publishing House, 1929; reprint, 1986), 273.

[24] Walther, *Justification—Objective and Subjective*, 12.

[25] Gerhard Friedrich Bente (1858–1930), quoted in: Rick Curia, *History of Objective or Universal Justification*, 61.

We are saved by Christ through faith, not through Christ by our faith. The order and basis for our justification must be explicitly connected to the incarnate Christ's actions on earth in these the last days. "The ground [of justification] lies alone in the merit of Christ, for by this our sins are blotted out, and God is enabled to receive us again into favor. The means, however, through which we attain justification is faith."[26]

Faith is personal, but justification—the righteousness given in the Gospel—is of a far greater scope. It is fine and salutary to talk about justification by faith, but to rule out any basis for justification outside of the personal puts one outside of Christian orthodoxy. If there is no real, earthly forgiveness outside the believing person, there is no actual forgiveness for the unbeliever to believe in. "Justification must previously exist before it can be accepted by faith," while the reverse position must "regard faith as the efficient cause of justification."[27] "He who believes does not first make reality of something that God had only made possible, but recognizes and confirms what, on the side of God, was long truth and reality. He who does not believe renders impotent and invalid what was already reality."[28] Justification by faith, a truly biblical teaching, "would be impossible, if the world had not first been justified by the death and resurrection of Christ, and if Christ's condemnation in death had not been followed by His absolution in the resurrection."[29] Justification is not made by faith: it is *offered* before faith in the Gospel and *received* in faith as the Gospel comes. This is the historic Lutheran teaching: "Faith justifies not by itself, by its own dignity or value, by moving God to justify the believer, but because, as an instrument or receptive means, it lays hold of the merit of Christ," that is, the forgiveness that is offered in the Gospel.[30]

Faith does not change God; rather, it receives the gracious God, who is already reconciled to mankind in His Son. Faith is having the right

---

[26] Heinrich Schmid, *The Doctrinal Theology of the Evangelical Lutheran Church*, 425.

[27] Discussion of theses accepted at the first convention of the Synodical Conference (1872), quoted in: Rick Curia, *History of Objective or Universal Justification*, 40.

[28] George Stoeckhardt, "General Justification," 143–44.

[29] Reinhold Pieper (1850–1920), "Theses Concerning Justification," Wisconsin Synod Convention (1879–1880), quoted in: Rick Curia, *History of Objective or Universal Justification*, 39.

[30] David Hollaz, quoted in: Heinrich Schmid, *The Doctrinal Theology of the Evangelical Lutheran Church*, 436.

God—the Father who loves, forgives, and is revealed in Christ. "Faith neither creates something new, nor does it cause something to happen, in the effective sense. Faith is not an agent for salvation, justification, or forgiveness. The role of faith is exclusively instrumental, in which role it appropriates something that already exists."[31] If Christ's work does not affect the new relationship of God to the world, then nothing is left to bring about this change except faith. Forgiving sins—preaching faith in Christ—is not a sacrificial work to move the wrathful God towards man: He is already a kind and loving Father. Therefore, faith, the reception of Christ, must be distinguished from its basis. Because the "the ground of justification is exterior to man,"[32] "Therefore the nature of faith as it has to do with justification (*fides justificans*) is apprehension, receptivity, or the application of the promise of grace, according to the language of Scripture."[33] If the basis of justification is what goes on inside man, we are left without real comfort because "terrified minds seek consolation outside of themselves," namely, the promise that justifies.[34]

While the varying human formulations might seem abstract and academic, this aspect of justification determines what is preached and what is believed. "And we know that all, also what is said concerning general (universal) justification, was written for our comfort and serves our salvation."[35] If faith is a work, the promise is a conditional offer that *demands* something. A free offer of salvation with a hook—an unmet term—removes actual forgiveness from the Gospel. "If justification is not universal and objective, then it is only individual and subjective. Preaching forgiveness that only becomes real when faith is added already confuses law and gospel, and as soon as forgiveness depends upon something in the sinner it's only a matter of time before other conditions of the law are attached."[36]

---

[31] Jon Buchholz, "Jesus Canceled Your Debt!," 32.

[32] Heinrich Schmid, *The Doctrinal Theology of the Evangelical Lutheran Church*, 434.

[33] Chemnitz, *Loci Theologici* (1653), quoted in: Robert Preus, "Justification as Taught by Post-Reformation Lutheran Theologians," 16.

[34] Melanchthon, *Loci Communes*, quoted in: Heinrich Schmid, *The Doctrinal Theology of the Evangelical Lutheran Church*, 434.

[35] George Stoeckhardt, "General Justification," 144.

[36] Jon Buchholz, "Jesus Canceled Your Debt!," 30.

Where the objective emphasis on God's reconciliation is not denied, it can be charitably assumed. The Gospel can be purely preached so that sins are forgiven without talking about faith, and so also, without detailing the basis for it in objective justification. In either case, Christ's work must touch the unbeliever before faith can be created by the Spirit. "Since we receive remission of sins and the Holy Ghost by faith alone, faith alone justifies, because those reconciled are accounted righteous and children of God, not on account of their own purity, but through mercy for Christ's sake, provided only they by faith apprehend this mercy" (Ap 4:86). Faith does not take an active role in creating salvation, but something must. Rather, faith receives what is objectively there, what has been finalized in Christ's resurrection. The refusal to discuss justification in itself, apart from faith, means faith (or rather, man's works) takes over the role of Christ in justification.

Is there forgiveness without faith? If not, the Gospel has nothing in it: it is devoid of forgiveness, so that Christ becomes entirely dependent on man's potential faith to justify. What is the power of the Gospel? Saying "justification by faith" does not address what God gives and offers before man believes. The fact that only believers are imputed with Christ's righteousness does not address the critical matter of how and why man comes to be justified by Christ.

Chapter 19

Isaac Barrow: A Historical Witness

Although known today for his mathematical and natural science contributions in the 17th century, Isaac Barrow (1630–1677) has a fascinating story. As a mathematics professor who furthered the nascent field of calculus, he taught a young Isaac Newton, and even though he gave up his professorship to Newton to pursue theology, he was still one of the greatest scientific minds in England. This ordained Greek scholar and mathematician became a well-regarded Anglican churchman and theologian, devoting himself entirely to churchly pursuits in the latter part of his earthly life. The probing theological works of this royal chaplain were republished regularly for 200 years. The fact that he wrote in English removes the complication of translation.

A particular sermon of Barrow's on the resurrection of Christ provides an interesting datapoint for the topic of objective justification. This Anglican highlights themes that were not hotly debated at the time. Barrow makes various points about the necessity and value of the resurrection of our Lord. He starts with how Jesus' resurrection highlights the truthfulness of God—the keeping of His promises and prophecies. Next, Barrow shows how the resurrection proves all the teaching of Christ and displays His character and divine nature. The next point takes up a large portion of the sermon. It deals with "the efficacy of his undertakings for us."[1] Barrow especially addresses the objective aspect of justification in this extended treatment of the result of Christ's finished work.

Using many of the scriptural passages highlighting the objective aspect of justification, Barrow systematically details the immediate benefits of Christ's resurrection:

> for considering it we may not doubt of God's being reconciled to us, of obtaining pardon of our sins and acceptance of our persons, of receiving all helps conducible to our sanctification, of attaining final happiness, in case we are not on our parts deficient; all those benefits by our Lord's resurrection, as a certain seal, being ratified to us, and in a manner conferred on us.[2]

The matters he discussed are of benefit, of course, only to individuals who believe, but he expounds on what follows from the resurrection of Christ for all mankind. By considering what happened as a result of His resurrection, Barrow details what mankind actually receives from Christ, apart from any one person. God is reconciled and forgiveness is conferred objectively upon humanity in Christ's resurrection.

The payment for our sin Christ made is parallel to our acceptance in the Lord's rising: "in raising him thence correspondency God did express himself appeased, and his law to be satisfied." This acceptance of Christ was done on our behalf, just as with His death, so that He

> was solemnly reinstated in favour, and we representatively, or virtually, in him so that (supposing our due qualifications and the performances requisite on our parts) we thence become completely justified, having not only a just title to what justification doth import, but a real instatement therein, confirmed by the resurrection of our Saviour.

Barrow concludes, after citing Rom. 4:25 and Rom. 8:33 34:

> our justification and absolution are, ye see, rather ascribed to the resurrection of Christ, than to his death for that indeed his death was the ground of bestowing them, but his resurrection did accomplish the collation [conferral] of them for since (doth the apostle argue) God hath acknowledged satisfaction done to his justice by discharging our surety

---

[1]Isaac Barrow, "The Christian Faith Explained and Vindicated," in *The Works of Isaac Barrow,* vol. 2, eds. Abraham Hill and James Hamilton (New York: John C. Riker, 1845; http://archive.org/details/worksofisaacbarr02barr), 496.

[2]Isaac Barrow, "The Christian Faith Explained and Vindicated," 496.

from restraint and from all further prosecution; since in a manner so notorious God hath declared his favour toward our proxy; what pretence can be alleged against us, what suspicion of displeasure can remain? Had Christ only died, we should not have been condemned, our punishment being already undergone; yet had we not been fully discharged, without that express warrant and acquittance which his rising doth imply: so again may St. Paul be understood to intimate, when he saith, *If Christ be not raised, your faith is vain; ye are yet in your sins:* death . . . was condemned, and judicially abolished, by his death; but it was executed and expunged in his resurrection. . . . [3]

This passage makes a sharp distinction between the work of Christ proper and its approval by the Father. Christ as our proxy and representative was approved for our sake, so we, that is sinful mankind, are "virtually" justified in Christ. This real conferral is in our surety: Christ, the one who took our debt. As another theologian states: "He was not exposed to suffering indirectly or incidentally, but in a direct and immediate way, as our representative."[4] "Christ redeemed us from the curse of the law by becoming a curse for us" (Gal. 3:13). Also, Is. 53 clearly speaks of the substitutionary nature of His suffering and death. The Lord's resurrection is not less substitutionary than His death.

The description of Christ as our surety, the one imputed with our sins, is also found in Lutheranism:

He paid by His Passion and death all the penalties which were owed by those who transgressed the Law. God imputed our obligations to His Son as to our Surety and Bondsman. On the basis of the Law God required from Him, as the one standing surety for the accused, the due penalties of sin. The Son voluntarily put Himself at the disposal of God the Father (Ps. 40:10, 11; Heb. 10:7, 9) and in our stead and place made Himself a bondsman on behalf of sinful man and a debtor. He took our cause upon Himself, that is, He undertook to pay all the debts of the world and to expiate all its sins. Thus the curse of the Law was not directed against the one who deserved it, but by an imputation arising from His suretyship against the One who took up our cause, and He truly felt and experienced that divine curse.[5]

---

[3]Isaac Barrow, "The Christian Faith Explained and Vindicated," 496.

[4]George Smeaton, *The Doctrine of the Atonement as Taught by the Apostles*, 77.

[5]Quenstedt, quoted in: Robert Preus, "Justification as Taught by Post-Reformation Lutheran Theologians," 4.

While this is not justification in itself, this imputation to Christ means that Christ's absolution, as our surety, is also our reconciliation, the "non-imputing of sins" (2 Cor. 5:19). "And because Christ lived, died, and was raised as our representative substitute, his perfect obedience is credited to us, his penalty-bearing death counts for us, and his justifying resurrection is the Lord's approval of all of us who trust in the righteous Son."[6] While Calvinists, as displayed the former quote, limit objective justification to believers, Lutherans confess that Christ's resurrection is effective for the whole world.

The resurrection of our representative is the completion of salvation. From the side of God, He is completely reconciled, and there can be no more prosecution or allegation by the Father. Barrow clearly separates the death and resurrection in a biblical manner: Christ's death is the "ground," that is, the required payment of redemption, but His resurrection actually secures, ratifies, and discharges our debt of sin and demonstrates publicly the world's reception into God's favor.

To show that he is not inventing anything new, Barrow includes a chain of quotes from early theologians to back his point that Christ's resurrection has a universal effect *before* man comes into the picture:

> [Christ] (saith St. Chrysostom) *by his resurrection dissolved the tyranny of death, and with himself raised up the whole world; By the pledge of his resurrection* (saith St. Ambrose) *he loosed the bands of hell; Thereby* (saith St. Leo) *death received its destruction and life its beginning.*[7]

This objective aspect has long been expressed, but more in passing until the modern era, since it was already implicit in every statement of the Gospel.

Next, to put into perspective the objective aspect, Barrow shows how this virtual justification of mankind in Christ comes in the means of grace: "Hence in our baptism (wherein justification and a title to eternal life are exhibited to us) as the death and burial of Christ are symbolically undergone by us; so therein also we do interpretatively rise with him."[8] This follows the logic of Rom. 6:3–4: "Do you not know that all of us who have been baptized into Christ Jesus were baptized into

---

[6] Lee Tankersley, "Raised for Our Justification."

[7] Isaac Barrow, "The Christian Faith Explained and Vindicated," 496–97.

[8] Isaac Barrow, "The Christian Faith Explained and Vindicated," 497.

his death? We were buried therefore with him by baptism into death, in order that, just as Christ was raised from the dead by the glory of the Father, we too might walk in newness of life." Here the subjective aspect of justification connects with the objective. Justification, which is ours virtually in Christ, is truly given in Baptism—a form of the forgiving Gospel. What is complete and objectively true in Christ causes man to rise with Christ in faith, receiving all the benefits of the Lord's resurrection.

Justification is presented not as a possibility, but as an actual gift that is "exhibited" to sinners in Baptism. It exists before its reception, since Baptism itself is given before man trusts in its promise. The blessings which flow directly from Christ's resurrection are not apart from forgiveness, but manifested in it. Barrow concludes this subsection:

> Nor is it strange, that to the hearty belief and ingenuous profession of this one article (it enfolding or inferring the truth of all other Christian doctrines), salvation is annexed, according to that assertion of St. Paul: *The righteousness of faith saith thus* (or this is the purport of the Christian institution) *that if thou shalt confess with thy mouth the Lord Jesus, and shalt believe in thy heart that God raised him from the dead, thou shalt be saved.*[9]

Salvation is not just *potentially* true, it is "annexed"—fully appropriated by Christ on our behalf. This is much more than a payment that makes salvation possible: salvation is fully achieved.

Barrow, quite eloquently, uses the objective aspect of justification in the most Christian way: to comfort sinners with the objective forgiveness with which Christ's resurrection empowers the Gospel.

> Surely, by this noble experiment [the public resurrection of Christ] we are clearly informed and should be fully persuaded, that nothing can destroy us, nothing can harm us, nothing can separate us from our God and our happiness that no force, no fraud, no spite of men, or rage of hell, can finally prevail against us what, then, reasonably can be dreadful or discouraging to us, what should be able to drive us into distrust or despair?[10]

God's acceptance, His full justification of sinners, is already accomplished and resides for us in Christ. Our comfort is never found in ourselves, but

---

[9]Isaac Barrow, "The Christian Faith Explained and Vindicated," 498.

[10]Isaac Barrow, "The Christian Faith Explained and Vindicated," 499.

in the one who was absolved—not just for Himself, but for all mankind.

Yet, Barrow does not leave this truth to be taken for granted, without a real call to repentance. He concludes with the reception of justification from man's side, completing the picture:

> Our Lord did by his resurrection gain a dominion over us, unto which if we do not submit, we shall be very injurious and wicked . . . if we defeat that gracious purpose: it is the condition of our obtaining the happy fruits and benefits of his resurrection, that we should ourselves rise with him unto righteousness and newness of life by not complying therewith, we shall render his resurrection unprofitable to us, becoming unworthy and uncapable of any good advantage thereby.[11]

While justification is complete from God's side, man rejects this in unbelief. Scripture details how man must continually turn from sin and die to it:

> *Awake* (saith the apostle) *thou that sleepest, and arise from the dead, and Christ shall give thee life;* to awake from our spiritual slumber, to arise from dead works, are the terms on which Christ doth offer that eternal happy life: for as the pains and ignominies of his death will nowise avail those who are not conformable to his death, in dying to sin and mortifying their lusts.[12]

No benefit is actually received without a turning away from sin and rising with Christ in faith. This truth of the subjective side of justification does not negate Christ's resurrection—or its effective power for mankind's absolution.

As forgiveness is in Christ, so God's wrath is a constant threat for all those living in Adam:

> our sins did slay him; it must be our repentance that reviveth him to us, our obedience that maketh him to live [on] our behalf; for Christ is not in effect risen to impenitent people: as they continue dead in trespasses and sins, as they lie buried in corruption of heart and life, so their condemnation abideth, and death retaineth its entire power over them; they shall not καταντᾷν εἰς ἐξανάστασιν, attainment unto that happy resurrection, whereof our Lord's resurrection was the pledge and pattern; so did our Lord assure in his preaching: *He* (said our Lord) *that believeth in the Son* (that

---

[11]Isaac Barrow, "The Christian Faith Explained and Vindicated," 500.

[12]Isaac Barrow, "The Christian Faith Explained and Vindicated," 500.

is, who with a sincere, strong, and lively faith, productive of due obedience, believeth in him) *hath everlasting life;* but ὁ ἀπειθῶν, *he that disobeyeth* (or with a practical infidelity disbelieveth) *the Son shall not see life, but the wrath of God abideth on him;* whence we may well infer with St. Paul, *Therefore, brethren, we are debtors, not to the flesh, to live after the flesh: for if we live after the flesh; we shall die; but if through the Spirit we do mortify the deeds of the body, we shall live;* that is, assuredly by obeying God's will we shall obtain, by disobedience we must forfeit, all the benefits of our Lord's resurrection.[13]

Barrow follows the scriptural pattern and demarcation of the twin aspects of salvation, without trying to play the universal benefit of Christ's resurrection against the individual's condemnation, repentance, and conversion. There is no contradiction between these within Scripture, and therefore there is none in doctrine.

This unique sermon by a respected and orthodox Anglican shows that this teaching is no mere invention of North American Lutherans, nor pietism.[14] Rather, it undergirds all Christian power in the Gospel itself. However, it has become more necessary to emphasize the objective aspect of justification as Christian theology has descended into the modern, unbiblical subjective regions—centering everything on the believer himself and his reaction to Christ, to the detriment of Christ's accomplished and effective work. Despite that, forgiveness, justification, and life still flow upon mankind in the word of reconciliation from Christ, our head and representative, in our virtual justification. What man does to deny or hide this great truth cannot undo what has already been done and declared in Christ.

---

[13] Isaac Barrow, "The Christian Faith Explained and Vindicated," 500.

[14] The first chapter of a raving book against objective justification is entitled: "The Age of Pietism Gave Us UOJ [Universal, Objective Justification]." Gregory Jackson, *Luther versus the Pietists*, 13.

Chapter 20

Confessional Evidence

For most of history, the objectivity of Christ's work, justification, forgiveness, and the Gospel was assumed and implicit, but that objectivity is denied in the modern age. Because there was no need to dwell on the distinction, or even clearly separate the objective and subjective aspects of justification, pre-modern theologians weaved them together most subtly and artfully. However, when we ask the right questions of the Lutheran Confessions, we find the objective aspect is pervasive throughout. This should be expected, since there is no real Gospel comfort for man without the objective reconciliation accomplished by Christ.

Asking for direct, historical proof to address a modern controversy is folly. The Reformers were faithful to Scripture, but their writings are not clairvoyant. We find they do not directly interact with controversies that arise after they were written. There is no article on the objective dimension of salvation in the Confessions, just as there is none on abortion or homosexuality or evolution; these were not issues the early Lutherans had to combat in their faithful confession of the truth.

While the Lutheran Confessions give a faithful confession of the doctrine of God's Word, they neither claim to be, nor are, an exhaustive summary of every possible heresy. A specific context and particular errors gave rise to them. Piecing doctrinal statements into a theological context helps us understand the aspects they most emphasized. The word "faith" was used by the Reformers to exclude works. How could they have foreseen that faith would become the preeminent work of those who claim the Reformation as their own, so that God-given faith is used to buy God's favor? Faith, as newly defined, has become the new indulgence within Protestantism.

The issue the first generation of Lutheran confessors tackled was the reception of Christ's salvation by the individual. It followed the biblical division of works versus faith.

> [The perfection of the world's redemption] was a given fact as far as Catholics and Lutherans were concerned. The primary point of contention between these two groups was in how the work of Christ for the world was brought to bear on the individual sinner.[1]

The Council of Trent, in reaction to Luther, doubled-down on its position. It legislated Rome's official stance:

> CANON XI. – If any one saith, that men are justified, either by the sole imputation of the justice of Christ, or by the sole remission of sins, to the exclusion of the grace and the charity which is poured forth in their hearts by the Holy Ghost, and is inherent in them; or even that the grace, whereby we are justified, is only the favour of God; let him be anathema.

> CANON XII. – If any one saith, that justifying faith is nothing else but confidence in the divine mercy which remits sins for Christ's sake; or, that this confidence alone is that whereby we are justified; let him be anathema.

> CANON XIII. – If any one saith, that it is necessary for every one, for the obtaining the remission of sins, that he believe for certain, and without any wavering arising from his own infirmity and disposition, that his sins are forgiven him; let him be anathema.[2]

As one scholar states, this context explains the subjective emphasis of the Confessions:

> It doesn't surprise us, then, that when the Lutheran Confessions treat the points of dispute [they] center largely on questions about how justification or the remission of sins are delivered to and obtained by the sinner. Therefore most of

---

[1] James F. Korthals, "Universal/Objective Justification: An Historical Perspective," Kettle Moraine Pastoral Conference, West Mequon, WI (Jan. 15 2013; http://essays.wls.wels.net/bitstream/handle/123456789/4143/KorthalsJustification.pdf), 5.

[2] Council of Trent, Sixth Session (1547; http://www.thecounciloftrent.com/ch6.htm).

the statements in the Lutheran Confessions and in writings
of Lutheran theologians during the Age of Orthodoxy deal
with the personal justification of an individual.[3]

However, a heavy emphasis on the subjective aspect is in no way a
denial of the objective scriptural aspect.

Consider what a modern, liberal Roman theologian has to say about
the concept of universal justification:

> what many Protestants call "justification" largely coincides
> with what we Catholics call "redemption" and many expres-
> sions that sound heretical ought to be understood as com-
> pletely orthodox . . . "*all* men are justified in Christ". . . . In
> ordinary Catholic usage—and in agreement with Scripture—
> this would mean nothing other than the totally orthodox
> statement that "*all men* are '*redeemed*' in or by Christ
> Jesus."[4]

While Rome and the Lutheran Confessions are not in agreement on
the personal side of justification, a 20th century Roman Catholic had
no problems with the teaching of objective justification. Even before
the American debate over objective justification began, a Romanizing
Anglican wrote: "To speak [of] our justification as the objective work of
Christ already accomplished, and to say that the formal cause of it is our
Lord's Resurrection just as the meritorious cause of it is His death . . .
no Christian denies it." This 1850 review then cites the Anglican turned
Roman (later Cardinal) John Henry Newman as evidence:

> he wrote on Justification, spoke of "the bold, nay correct,
> language of Luther, that Christ Himself is the form of our
> justification," and very similar language may be found in S.
> Thomas, and in Petavius. The question in dispute between
> Catholics and Protestants is not as to what Christ has done,
> but as to how what He has done takes effect upon us.[5]

So we should expect the Confessions to center less on the objective and
more on the personal side of justification, as they do. However, though
the term "objective justification" is not used, "our Confessions also
show that its writers had a concept and belief in the objective reality of
forgiveness and justification, before and apart from faith, as a result of

---

[3] James Korthals, "Universal/Objective Justification," 6.

[4] Hans Kueng, quoted in: Kurt Marquart, "Objective Justification," *Marquart's Works*, 6:75.

[5] "Smith's Inquiry Into Catholic Truths," in *The Theologian and Ecclesiastic*, 152–53.

Christ's work of redemption."[6]

The deniers of objective justification, however, take a flat view of history and misapply the marvelous confessional statements on subjective justification in order to denude the completed salvation the Lutheran Reformers successfully defended:

> When we hear the testimony of those of the era immediately following the Reformation, we rightly assume that they are more certain of what those writing, compiling, and teaching the Lutheran Symbols were asserting than those of later ages would be; that is, the presumption of accuracy is with those closest to the era or controversy unless and until proven otherwise.[7]

In spite of this non-Lutheran view of church tradition, the issue of objective justification is addressed competently by the Confessions, if we read them correctly: "The pattern is clear and consistent throughout [the Lutheran Confessions]: The Gospel or absolution offers not a conditional, future prospect, but a perfected, past and present reality."[8] Forgiveness is presented as ready-made in the Gospel, so that faith does not complete the work of Christ or make it effective. The entire Lutheran Confessions witness to this objective aspect, which made the Reformers confident enough to stand up to the entire world in their scriptural confession.

This reality and gift in the Gospel itself has been deemed a mere possibility by deniers of objective justification:

> It has been noted above that the Lutheran Confessions do speak of God being reconciled to men through Christ. They make clear their meaning, however, in so speaking, namely, that because of Christ's vicarious obedience God is able to be and is gracious and merciful to sinners; that He is able to and does grant forgiveness to the penitent.[9]

This approach leaves reconciliation incomplete, but the Confessions do speak objectively of the effects of Christ's work, as even a one-time denier of objective justification could admit:

> It may be noted here that the Lutheran Confessions do speak of Christ's sacrifice as propitiating God's wrath and of reconciling the Father to sinful humanity. See, e.g., Article III of the Augsburg Confession and Article XXIV, paragraph 19

---

[6]Rick Curia, *History of Objective or Universal Justification*, 13.

[7]ELDoNA, "Theses on the Article of Justification," 6.

[8]Kurt Marquart, "Objective Justification," *Marquart's Works*, 6:72.

[9]Maier, "A Summary Exposition of Justification," 26.

of the Apology. In using this terminology they communicate basic Biblical truth, indeed, but express themselves in a manner other than do the Scriptures. For example, Paul, in whose writings words of the *katallassoo* [to reconcile] family are found, nowhere uses the word "reconcile" (*katallassoo*) to state that Christ reconciled the Father to the world, or for that matter that God reconciled himself through Christ to the world of sinners.[10]

Of course, at stake is exactly what the highly significant word "reconcile" of 2 Cor. 5:19 teaches: "in Christ God was reconciling the world to himself, not counting their trespasses against them." This delves into the very nature of Christ's imputation. Christ did not just pay a debt abstractly; He took our sins and the wrath they merited.

He who takes upon himself the sins of the human race by bearing and carrying them and in this way removing them from us also takes upon himself the wrath of God and by that very act arouses the avenging justice of God against Himself. The reason for this is clear. The wrath of God follows upon all sins. Therefore where the universal weight of sin is fixed the weight of God's wrath also oppresses with its burden.[11]

Christ's death is the result of taking all of God's wrath, while His rising is the effacing of it for mankind in totality. God's wrath did not remain on Christ or condemn our Lord's body indefinitely; instead, our Father expressed Himself appeased and satisfied in raising Jesus.

The Confessions witness that Christ's reconciliation is complete, so that God's wrath is stilled in Christ. Many confessional examples of the benefits and efficiency of Christ's Word speak of a forgiveness-imparting, unconditional Gospel: "On account of [Christ], God has been placated,[12] reconciled,[13] and propitiated."[14] As a later theologian summarized: "As the atonement is a past accomplished fact, so is

---

[10]Maier, "A Summary Exposition of Justification," 34.

[11]John Dorsch (1683), quoted in: Robert Preus, "Justification as Taught by Post-Reformation Lutheran Theologians," 5.

[12]"AC XX 15, Lat., XXVII 49; Ap IV 87, 163, 222, 230, 279, 292–93, 299; XII 80; XV 6."

[13]"Ap XXIV 38."

[14]"AC XX 24, Lat.; Ap IV 100, 180, 345, 379, XXIII 36." Ken R. Schurb, *Does the Lutheran Confessions' Emphasis on Subjective Justification Mitigate Their Teaching of Objective Justification?* (1982; http://archive.org/details/DoesTheLutheranConfessionsEmphasisOnSubjectiveJustificationMitigate), 21.

forgiveness, which is the result of the atonement, but the application (or we might say, the appropriation or actual having) of the work of Christ and its results occurs as the Spirit of God brings the individual to faith."[15] The treasures Christ already won are present objectively in the Gospel:

> These treasures are offered us by the Holy Ghost in the promise of the holy Gospel; and faith alone is the only means by which we lay hold upon, accept, and apply, and appropriate them to ourselves. This faith is a gift of God, by which we truly learn to know Christ, our Redeemer, in the Word of the Gospel, and trust in Him, that for the sake of His obedience alone we have the forgiveness of sins by grace, are regarded as godly and righteous by God the father, and are eternally saved. Therefore it is considered and understood to be the same thing when Paul says that we are justified by faith, Rom. 3:28, or that faith is counted to us for righteousness, Rom. 4:5, and when he says that we are made righteous by the obedience of One, Rom. 5:19, or that by the righteousness of One justification of faith came to all men, Rom. 5:18. For faith justifies, not for this cause and reason that it is so good a work and so fair a virtue, but because it lays hold of and accepts the merit of Christ in the promise of the holy Gospel; for this must be applied and appropriated to us by faith, if we are to be justified thereby. Therefore the righteousness which is imputed to faith or to the believer out of pure grace is the obedience, suffering, and resurrection of Christ, since He has made satisfaction for us to the Law, and paid for [expiated] our sins (*Formula of Concord* [FC] 3:10–14).

The subjective aspect of faith describes the appropriation of what is truly bestowed upon all in the Gospel. These are real treasures we receive, not empty chests we fill with faith. Faith is narrowly limited in this passage of the *Formula*—it has no virtuous or meritorious quality. It does not do anything for God—it is God's gift of forgiveness that changes man.

The 1529 *Schwabach Articles*, written primarily by Philipp Melanchthon and Martin Luther, were a precursor and source for the *Augsburg Confession*. They speak very clearly on the objective aspect of justification, even though, evidently, it was not as pertinent to the debate with Rome:

---

[15]Quenstedt, quoted in: Robert Preus, "Justification as Taught by Post-Reformation Lutheran Theologians," 10.

> Original sin is a real, genuine sin, not just a mistake or a weakness. Rather, this kind of sin condemns all people who stem from Adam and separates them from God eternally—If Jesus Christ had not intervened on our behalf and taken this sin and all sins that result from it upon himself. Through his suffering, he made satisfaction for this original sin and in himself completely removed and destroyed it as Psalm 50 and Romans 5 so clearly write about such sin.[16]

This document references Rom. 5, one of the key proofs of the objective aspect of justification. The reality of righteousness in Christ—where sin is entirely abolished—does not downplay the condemnation of sins in Adam.

What is true of the Word is also true of Baptism: faith clings to an objective treasure that is complete and applicable to all in Christ. What God gives is never an abstract gift that faith finishes wrapping. The only faith that saves is faith in Christ's promise, His perfected forgiveness.

> Now, they are so mad as to separate faith, and that to which faith clings and is bound, though it be something external. Yea, it shall and must be something external, that it may be apprehended by the senses, and understood and thereby be brought into the heart, as indeed the entire Gospel is an external, verbal preaching. In short, what God does and works in us He proposes to work through such external ordinances. Wherever, therefore, He speaks, yea, in whichever direction or by whatever means He speaks, thither faith must look, and to that it must hold. Now here we have the words: He that believeth and is baptized shall be saved. To what else do they refer than to Baptism, that is, to the water comprehended in God's ordinance? Hence it follows that whoever rejects Baptism rejects the Word of God, faith, and Christ, who directs us thither and binds us to Baptism (LC Bapt. 30–31).

Faith does not create a new uplink to God; instead, it holds to the already sufficient sacrifice of Christ, which gained remission for the entire world. The Confessions are replete with language that stresses that the gifts of Christ are ready-made. We may correctly say that the objective aspect of justification underlies every statement about faith's subjective receptivity. These two dimensions go hand-in-hand.

---

[16] Article IV. *Sources and Contexts of the Book of Concord,* eds. Robert Kolb and James A. Nestigen (Minneapolis: Augsburg Fortress, 2001), 85.

"The Lutheran Confessions teach objective justification, and this doctrine is neither restricted nor hindered by their teaching of subjective justification. To be sure, the Symbols say that 'all are justified'—in those precise syllables—only in SA II i 3. Still, the evidence in terms of such themes as forgiveness or reconciliation is massive."[17] Luther writes in the *Smalcald Articles,* as mentioned above, on the "The first and chief article:"

> That Jesus Christ, our God and Lord, died for our sins, and was raised again for our justification, Rom. 4:25. And He alone is the Lamb of God which taketh away the sins of the world, John 1:29; and God has laid upon Him the iniquities of us all, Is. 53:6. Likewise: All have sinned and are justified without merit by His grace, through the redemption that is in Christ Jesus, in His blood, Rom. 3:23f. Now, since it is necessary to believe this, and it cannot be otherwise acquired or apprehended by any work, law, or merit, it is clear and certain that this faith alone justifies us as St. Paul says, Rom. 3:28: For we conclude that a man is justified by faith, without the deeds of the Law. Likewise 3:26: That He might be just, and the Justifier of him which believeth in Christ.

According to Luther, justification is not less real than sin: "All have sinned and are justified." This dual truth precedes, and is necessary to promote, the truth of justification by faith alone, so that faith and salvation do not become cursed works of man.

One of the most clear and simple passages of the Confessions stressing that forgiveness precedes faith is almost too obvious: "We receive absolution, that is, forgiveness, from the pastor as from God Himself." This explanation of confession and absolution in the Small Catechism shows that faith receives salvation, so to have faith is to receive all the righteousness and forgiveness of Christ. Christ does not offer an incomplete, non-forgiving promise of salvation, and faith does not "finish baking the cake," so to speak. Forgiveness is ready-made, but still powerfully effective, in the Gospel. Faith receives these gifts—it does not distill them or synthesize them from the mere possibly of forgiveness merited by Christ.

The Lutheran Confessions speak more carefully of faith than do the modern deniers of objective justification: "And, again, as often as

---

[17]Ken Schurb, *Lutheran Confessions' Emphasis on Subjective Justification,* 57.

we speak of faith, we wish an object to be understood, namely, the promised mercy" (Ap 4:55). To have faith is to have what is promised—the forgiveness of sins. "Faith is the human side of justification, while justification is the divine side of faith. It is in this sense that faith has no dimension but exists only as the means of justification."[18]

Genuine Lutherans have always held that the Confessions "expressly teach that justification and remission of sins is the same thing."[19] Forgiveness is received in faith, but given to all in the Gospel, since it exists and has been enacted and declared in Christ: "that for His sake they freely receive remission of sins and reconciliation" (Ap 4:18). While the merits of Christ are inert for the deniers of objective justification today, that was not the case for early Lutherans. The merits of Christ are not just the payment, but also include its acceptance—the absolution of all sin in Christ by the Father. So the merits of Christ—His benefits—are truly given and received in the Gospel itself. Faith is instrumental in justification, the Confessions clearly delineate. It does not jump a metaphorical chasm between Christ's death and the believer by animating the Gospel.

God is reconciled completely, according to Lutheran teaching. This reconciliation is not for a select few, but applies to all the world. This objective fact is a large part of the Gospel:

> That the human race is truly redeemed and reconciled with God through Christ, who, by His faultless obedience, suffering, and death, has merited for us the righteousness which avails before God, and eternal life. That such merit and benefits of Christ shall be presented, offered, and distributed to us through His Word and Sacraments (FC SD 11:15–16).

The objective reality of forgiveness, often historically conflated with the atonement, is what is now called objective justification: "by his death 'our sins are blotted out';" "God has been reconciled to us because of Christ's suffering" (Ap 4:382). Faith does not complete this reconciliation—Christ already did for us. "For faith does not justify or save because it is a worthy work in and of itself, but only because it receives the promised mercy" (Ap 4:56) "For to believe means to receive

---

[18] Martim Warth, "Justification through Faith in Article Four of the Apology," 118.

[19] Discussion of theses accepted at the first convention of the Synodical Conference (1872), quoted in: Rick Curia, *History of Objective or Universal Justification*, 40.

what is there."[20]

The early church father Ambrose (337–397) is both a confessional and an early historical source for objective justification, since he is quoted in the *Apology to the Augsburg Confession* 4:103–105:

> Here and there among the Fathers similar testimonies are extant. For Ambrose says in his letter to a certain Irenaeus: Moreover, the world was subject to Him by the Law for the reason that, according to the command of the Law, all are indicted, and yet, by the works of the Law, no one is justified, i.e., because, by the Law, sin is perceived, but guilt is not discharged. The Law, which made all sinners, seemed to have done injury, but when the Lord Jesus Christ came, He forgave to all sin which no one could avoid, and, by the shedding of His own blood, blotted out the handwriting which was against us. This is what he says in Rom. 5:20: "The Law entered that the offense might abound. But where sin abounded, grace did much more abound." Because after the whole world became subject, He took away the sin of the whole world, as he [John] testified, saying: "Behold the Lamb of God, which taketh away the sin of the world." And on this account let no one boast of works, because no one is justified by his deeds. But he who is righteous has it given him because he was justified after the laver [of Baptism]. Faith, therefore, is that which frees through the blood of Christ, because he is blessed "whose transgression is forgiven, whose sin is covered," Ps. 32:1. These are the words of Ambrose, which clearly favor our doctrine; he denies justification to works, and ascribes to faith that it sets us free through the blood of Christ. Let all the Sententiarists, who are adorned with magnificent titles, be collected into one heap. For some are called angelic; others, subtile, and others irrefragable [that is, doctors who cannot err.] When all these have been read and reread, they will not be of as much aid for understanding Paul as is this one passage of Ambrose.

After acknowledging that all are sinners and no one is justified in Adam, Ambrose states that Christ "forgave to all sin which no one could avoid." This forgiveness to all is a clear proclamation of objective justification in the Confessions. It is an unambiguous reference to Rom. 5, where Christ's work of justification parallels Adam's sin, which gave birth to condemnation for all. Yet, since this contradicts the assumptions of some, these words are reinterpreted.

---

[20]F. Pieper, "Walther as Theologian: Justification, Universal," 4.

This Ambrose quote has been frequently used since Walther's time,[21] but Rydecki gloats: "you have found one paragraph in the Apology (IV:103) that does use the words 'forgave' and 'all' in the same sentence?"[22] All are forgiven through Christ's work, but only believers receive it. It is not illogical, but Rydecki can only see a contradiction. Ambrose sees both Adam's sin as universal, and what happened to sin in Christ: "all are indicted . . . no one is justified" by "the Law, which made all sinners." Thankfully, sin is not greater than Christ and what He has fully accomplished: "because after the whole world became subject, He took away the sin of the whole world." Only a hatred of the true Gospel could make Christ's benefits less universal than Adam's curse.

The larger argument of justification by faith supposedly rules out talking about the basis for justification: what is prior to faith. "Such an interpretation [of Ambrose] ignores the context of the whole Article IV ("The Righteousness of Faith"), as well as the immediate context, the stated conclusion of Melanchthon."[23] Rydecki goes on to talk about faith and Baptism—undoing Ambrose's actual words: "Here Ambrose clearly states that the 'all' whose transgression is forgiven are the same 'all' who have been justified through Holy Baptism and faith."[24] But in the reception of Christ's forgiveness, indicated by the singular "he," Ambrose deftly transitions to the reception of it: "he who is righteous has it given him." There is clearly no contradiction for Ambrose to say Christ freed all men (in Himself) by His resurrection, and that men are (individually) freed when the Gospel (Baptism, in this case) is received and appropriated by faith.

Ambrose is not contradicting himself, nor was this text praised by the *Apology* because it was unclear or misleading. It speaks to the universality of both the law and the Gospel: "all are indicted." None are justified by the law, yet not all are personally condemned. All are forgiven, but that does not mean all accept it or come to faith. The "all indicted" matches the "forgave to all sin." The use of Jn. 1·29 cinches his argument that sin is no more on the world—it has been taken away.

---

[21]"Christ is the second Adam, what the Apology says is useful." Walther, *Justification—Objective and Subjective*, 9.

[22]Letter from Rydecki to President Jon Buchholz.

[23]Paul Rydecki, "The Forensic Appeal to the Throne of Grace," 33.

[24]Paul Rydecki, "The Forensic Appeal to the Throne of Grace," 34.

To say this confession of the universal forgiveness of Christ applies only to those who will come to faith is a direct contradiction of Ambrose's words and Scripture. It is a pure rationalization to say that "all" cannot mean "all," because it does not appear to be so. Yet the Scriptures, along with this testimony of Ambrose and the *Apology*, stand firm. Because no aspect of justification is allowed before faith, the deniers of objective justification must do Calvinistic gymnastics to explain this exceptionally clear passage of the *Apology*.

As the objective and subjective aspects of forgiveness are not conflated in the Confessions, neither are the law and the Gospel pitted against one another: "For the Gospel convicts all men that they are under sin, that they all are subject to eternal wrath and death, and offers, for Christ's sake, remission of sin and justification, which is received by faith" (Ap 4:62). While the Confessions do not thoroughly debunk every modern argument of those who think forgiveness is not real until faith comes to animate Christ's forgiveness, their position is clear. It takes only one positive example to prove that the Lutheran Confessions do not deny the objective justification which resides in Christ, but let this truth of Scripture inform the power of the Gospel they so clearly articulate.

Chapter 21

Lutheran Dogmaticians

Quite curiously, the writings of orthodox Lutheran theologians, not the Confessions of the Lutheran Church, are frequently the battleground on which the validity of objective justification is fought. This is strange for those who define Lutheranism by the *Book of Concord*, not the tradition of those who followed it. Yet, those who come immediately after the Confessions do not deny the objective aspect they confess.

The preface to ELDoNA's theses already brings up the Lutheran fathers:

> A pastor was recently removed from a church body's clergy roster, ostensibly for false doctrine concerning the Article of Justification. His statements concerning this article of doctrine were entirely compatible with the fathers of Lutheran orthodoxy, but were considered "inadequate," because they did not fully express certain formulations demanded by said church body.

They footnote the period of their "fathers" with precision: "By this phrase, we are restricting our present consideration to the period beginning with Martin Luther and ending with Johann Gerhard (c. AD 1515–1637)."[1] However, it is artificially limiting to use only theologians who came before the subjectivism of pietism and the Enlightenment. Objective justification is said to be "based on questionable exegesis that would be foreign to the early Lutherans."[2] But the tenor of their

---

[1] ELDoNA, "Theses on the Article of Justification," 1.

[2] Eric Stefanski, "Theses on the Article of Justification: A Refutation of the ACLC's Critique: Part One."

teaching is clear, including on this issue of the basis for justification by faith. They do not speak in so many words on objective justification, but the reality of forgiveness and the inherent power of the Gospel, apart from faith, is evident throughout Lutheranism—until more modern times, that is.

Lutherans have always understood the Gospel as forgiveness itself. Perhaps because of their method, the Lutheran dogmaticians may not have emphasized the effective power of the Gospel as clearly as Luther did, but for them justification, nonetheless, was not an imaginary concept until faith is worked in a believer by the Spirit. This is a basic Lutheran tenet: "forgiveness is an objective fact, entirely independent of whether the sinner believes or not."[3]

The freedom of forgiveness and the defeat of sin are objectively true, and this verdict in Christ allows these benefits to be received in faith. The opposing side counters: "We condemn every form of universalism and any thought that man has the merit and righteousness of Christ applied to him other than through that faith which is created by these *media salutis* [means of salvation]."[4] The problem with this is that the application of Gospel depends on that which is before faith. Talking about the reception of salvation and insinuating universalism is beside the point. The Lutheran dogmaticians acknowledged the universal benefits of Christ:

> And by fulfilling that Law perfectly and by suffering all punishment He presented an obedience to divine righteousness which was sufficient to the last ounce (*ex asse*) and also freed us from the wrath of God, the curse of the Law, from sin and all evil. This obedience He now offers God the Father, and by His intercession He obtains everything good and needful for us.[5]

Since God is reconciled by Christ, the wrath of God is not applied in Christ.

Christ "offers to the world, through the Word of the Gospel, the benefits obtained by His suffering and death, applies them to believers,

---

[3]Martin Diers, "Objective Justification," 3.

[4]ELDoNA, "Theses on the Article of Justification," 3.

[5]Quenstedt, quoted in: Robert Preus, "Justification as Taught by Post-Reformation Lutheran Theologians," 4.

and in this way justifies them."[6] Something is actually offered in the Gospel, termed here the "benefits:" the fruit of the atonement, none other than justification. Absolution applies "the merits and benefits of Christ for the forgiveness of sins."[7] This is what objective justification confesses against the "faith" of Gospel receptionism: the reality of actual forgiveness in the Gospel. Logically, faith comes after Gospel, but if forgiveness comes after faith, then faith makes effective Christ's merits. Thus, faith moves God and propitiates His wrath, activating and actually cashing in Christ's merits. That is not the case, however: justification is already in effect for all—the payment to God was accepted and Christ was absolved in the stead of all.

John Gerhard precisely states:

> As God punished our sins in Christ, because they were laid on Him and imputed to Him as our Substitute, so in the same manner [the Father], by raising [Christ] from the dead, absolved Him by this very act [of resurrection] of our sins which had been imputed to Him, and thereby [the Father] absolved us in [Christ] also.[8]

This spectacular quote has been attacked by many deniers of objective justification:

> [Rune] Söderlund [in 1979] attacks Biblicum's ["an independent Lutheran theological institution in Sweden"] use of the Calov quote from *Biblia Illustrata* on Romans 4:25, which says either that God absolved us in him or absolves us in him. According to Söderlund as well as Rydecki and ELDoNA, *absolvit* [in Latin] should be translated in the present tense,[9]

so that God did not absolve (past tense) at the resurrection, but only in the present as men come to faith. But the words clearly say "in Christ," tying the two acts together. It cannot be the case that Christ is absolved whenever we believe. Rather, the one, singular act of justification—in Christ—is justification for all.

Later Lutheran theologians, when the pietistic emphasis on the

---

[6]Gerhard, quoted in: Paul Rydecki, "The Forensic Appeal to the Throne of Grace," 36.

[7]Martin Chemnitz, *Examination of the Council of Trent,* trans. Fred Kramer (St. Louis: Concordia Publishing House, 1978), 2:575.

[8]Walther, *Justification—Objective and Subjective,* 21.

[9]Magnus Sørensen, "The Justification of Christ," 13, 15.

subjective increased, spoke more emphatically about the objective aspect of justification. Johann Jacob Quistorp (1717–1766) wrote:

> The word Justification, as well as the word Reconciliation, is employed in a two-fold manner: 1. in regard to the acquired merit; 2. in regard to the appropriated merit. Thus *all* are justified (in one sense) and *some* are justified (in another sense). All, namely with respect to the acquired merit; and some, namely, with respect to the appropriated merit.[10]

This exceptionally clear text fully lays out the matter. A reconciliation was accomplished, having been declared at Christ's resurrection.

> However, we are said to be reconciled to God both because He is the offended and we the offending party, and because the origin and source of reconciliation is to be found in God and not in us. Thus it is necessary for us that we be reconciled to Him whom we have offended (Matt. 5:23) just as a woman ought to be reconciled with a man whom she has irritated (I Cor. 7:11). . . . This reconciliation has nothing to do with conversion and renewal of life.[11]

A past event provided the new relationship between God and world—one of reconciliation—so that, in Christ, all are absolved, and no wrath exists towards mankind.

The tie between our justification in Christ and His physical resurrection was made explicit long before the 19th century. Godfrey Olearius (d. 1715) makes that very connection:

> That Christ paid for us what He had pledged Himself to pay, and that His payment was sufficient, His resurrection demonstrated, since it shows that our surety has been absolved, the obligation which He has assumed having been annulled by His satisfaction, and hence we are together with Him justified in the judgment of God.[12]

"Christ's resurrection was necessary for our justification for other reasons," including:

> *the actual absolution from sins.* Just as God punished our sins in Christ, which were placed on him and imputed to him as our Bondsman; so also by the very act of raising him from the dead, God absolved Christ of our sins, which were imputed to him. So for that reason, God also absolved

---

[10]Quoted in: Rick Curia, *History of Objective or Universal Justification*, 23.

[11]Quensted, quoted in: Robert Preus, "Justification as Taught by Post-Reformation Lutheran Theologians," 5.

[12]Quoted in: Rick Curia, *History of Objective or Universal Justification*, 27.

us in Christ (Cf. 1 Corinthians 15:17; 2 Corinthians 5:21; Ephesians 2:5; Galatians 2:12–13; Philippians 3:8–10; 1 Peter 1:3).[13]

This small selection of evidence shows that this teaching of objective justification is not the property of any one church body: it is a regular part of Lutheran dogmatic presentations. It follows, as expected, from what Luther most powerfully taught and the Lutheran Confessions codified.

---

[13] Abraham Calov, "Selections from Abraham Calov's *Biblia Illustrata*," 23.

Chapter 22

Practical Denials of Objective Justification

The Gospel is indiscriminate in its application. It offers what is objectively there: a judgment upon the world in Christ. "When the pastor absolves he distributes a treasure which is already at hand, namely the forgiveness of sins which has already been gained."[1] While many do not take issue with the dogmatic formulation of objective justification, its practical denial is endemic. Wherever the forgiveness of the Gospel is made conditional or theoretical, there the justification declared in Christ is left in the tomb.

To make forgiveness dependent on a person, or his faith, is to direct a sinner to his own heart, which pulls him away from the Gospel of Christ. Here is one example of a sermon that assumes the idea of the Gospel, but does not actually give it: "Repent of your worry and all your idolatries and all your sins and look to Christ for forgiveness and righteousness, because your heavenly Father promises forgiveness to all who trust in Christ."[2] A Gospel that is only a signpost to a possible future action by God is not the forgiving Gospel, but a human message incapable of forgiving real sins. Luther already exposed this error: "For [the pope's forgiveness] is a *conditionalis clavis,* a conditional, a vacillating key which does not direct us to God's Word, but to our own repentance."

---

[1]F. Pieper, "Walther as Theologian: Justification, Universal," 4.
[2]Paul Rydecki, "Worry is Idolatrous, Useless, and Needless" (Sept. 9, 2018; http://www.godwithuslc.org/worry-is-idolatrous-useless-and-needless).

"An uncertain absolution is none at all. Indeed it is equivalent to lying and deception."[3] The Gospel, in practice, is too often other-worldly and inaccessible to those weak on objective justification.

For many modern Lutherans faith takes a place alongside Christ's work, completely redefining the nature of the promise. Follow this reasoning of a Lutheran theologian:

> In connection with the so-called general absolution, this retention [of sins] should always be used: since otherwise, in a mixed assembly composed of both classes, the promises of the gospel are applied without discrimination, and while comforting believers, may serve also to harden hypocrites, who have need of the law, instead of the Gospel.[4]

The Gospel, for fear of abuse, is never supposed to be given undiluted— it must always be conditioned by the law—because not all will believe. But if the promise demands anything from man, it is of the law and not the true Gospel. If forgiveness is limited, then forgiveness is not readily available—objective justification has been denied. In this rejection, the Gospel must become less than the forgiveness of sins.

Consider this egregious denial of objective justification:

> In the majority of cases the frail consciences of men have been appeased by the simple deception of imagining the Preparatory Rite in the Divine Service to be the Holy Absolution. It is even labeled as such in Lutheran hymnals! But technically, it is not really an absolution, an actual removal of sins. In the first place, an absolution cannot be spoken over a group. But even more significantly, an absolution can never be spoken over unexamined penitents. The absolution spoken in the Preparatory Rite is a reminder of God's grace, as assurance that God forgives the sins of the penitent believers for Jesus' sake. The promise there proclaimed is valid: our sins are forgiven for Jesus' sake. Christians are not required to confess their sins to the pastors in order to be forgiven by God. But if the Christian is to receive Absolution as it has been instituted by God, from the pastor, he needs first to confess to the pastor.[5]

---

[3]Luther, "The Keys" (1530), LW 40:367, 344.

[4]Henry E. Jacobs, "Retention of Sins," in *The Lutheran Cyclopedia,* eds. H. E. Jacobs and John A. W. Haas (New York: Charles Scribner's Sons, 1899), 409.

[5]David Petersen, "How to Make Confession: Just Do It," *Gottesdienst* 15:1 (2007; http://www.gottesdienst.org/gottesblog/2018/10/24/tbt-how-to-make-confession-just-do-it), 11.

Here, absolution becomes something much narrower than the Gospel. If the Gospel cannot be spoken to a group, preaching would be a waste of time. The high-church attempt to uplift the office of the ministry—at the expense of Christ's forgiveness—is satanic. The absolution given privately is a truly forgiving word, but so is the public proclamation of the Gospel—both flow from Christ who is risen. "Those, however, who simply take away and condemn the use of private absolution, err. But also those who contend that by the general proclamation of the Gospel sins are forgiven to no one, but that forgiveness takes place only in private absolution."[6]

The power of the Gospel and its absolving effect have long been the central battle line in Lutheranism.

> By private absolution, no essentially different or better for-giveness is imparted than in the preaching of the Gospel. Neither is it in such a way necessary for receiving forgiveness that without it no forgiveness of sins would take place. Still it has its own peculiar value and usefulness, because by it the individual is made more certain that he also has the forgiveness of sins.[7]

The early purveyors of objective justification were defining the Gospel and its inherent power against those who, while claiming the name Lutheran, made Christianity a religion of man's response: Absolution "is a ceremonial, always valid declaration of God through the mouth of the minister that he, then and there will . . . cancel and truly cancels all guilt and punishment only in so far as a man truly believes in Christ as he confesses [he does]."[8] This same error of making the absolution of Christ an inert ceremony—based on the performance of a certain man instead of a living power echoing throughout the church—is still alive and well.

Denial of objective justification was originally a claim that the Gospel was ineffective in itself. That is what started the controversy in earnest roughly 150 years ago:

---

[6]Chemnitz, *Examination of the Council of Trent*, 2:562.

[7]"Theodore Brohm, "[Intimate Connection of the Doctrine of Absolution with that of Justification]," quoted in: Rick Curia, *History of Objective or Universal Justification*, 15.

[8]Henry Allwardt (1889), quoted in: Rick Curia, *History of Objective or Universal Justification*, 53.

> In the 1860's and 70's, various individuals, particularly faculty members of Augsburg Theological Seminary, (then the de facto seminary of the Lutheran Free Church, a body which eventually merged into the ALC [and then the ELCA]), denied the efficacy of absolution. Their argument went as follows: Because no pastor can see the faith of anyone, he cannot know whether a person is truly justified.[9]

Whether it is the legalistic practice of private absolution or the teaching of the law itself that conditions the Gospel, this error obscures the fact that forgiveness is perfected and available in Christ.

> Private absolution is nothing else than the proclamation of the Gospel to the individual sinner. . . . It is contrary to Scripture and the pure Gospel to teach: That private absolution has, is based on, or confers some power outside the Gospel, e.g., a power inherent in the person or office of the person pronouncing the absolution.[10]

Christ did not command a specific rite of absolution, he gave the power of the keys to the church. They are certainly valid in private absolution, but to lift one mode of forgiveness above another is to make the objective justification of Christ conditional. Luther corrects this error: "Indeed if we have been absolved through the mouth of a brother or a minister, we must not look at the human being who is speaking. Nor should our eyes be directed toward danger and death."[11] Why the concern for the power of the Word of forgiveness? An uncertain absolution or Gospel is none at all. This is the modern works righteousness, the error which destroys churches and faith.

So while deniers of objective justification "vehemently deny being synergists," faith must do what Christ is said to have done in Scripture.[12] Faith is not called a work, but it must achieve something which Christ did not if justification only has to do with individuals that meet the criteria of faith. The Gospel does not have criteria though, "In [Christ] we have redemption through his blood, the forgiveness of our trespasses, according to the riches of his grace" (Eph. 1:7). The sure forgiveness found in Christ is what actually gives rise to faith. Faith is not a substance with which to bargain with God: it relies on Christ and

---

[9]Martin Diers, "Objective Justification," 3.

[10]CTCR, "Theses on Justification," 21.

[11]Luther, *Genesis Lectures* (1542), LW 5:130.

[12]Vernon Harley, "Synergism—Its Logical Association with General Justification."

receives the righteousness and absolution from His resurrection. If the absolution of the Gospel is not forgiveness, it is something less—and not of Christ.

If the objective dimension of forgiveness overtakes the subjective, however, faith becomes an abstraction. The power of faith is moved out of the present, and consequently, repentance over sins against God's righteousness is abstracted. The law is no longer used as a concrete power, but becomes a lifeless theory. This may not be a widespread academic error in the LCMS currently, but a lack of attention to the power of the Gospel has been displayed in actual preaching.

Without an objective law and an objective Gospel, there can be no boldness, no speaking either divine verdict in God's stead. What is left is merely human attempts to grasp at the divine and feebly describe it. These divine powers, verdicts, and sentences, though, are to be applied without equalization or balancing, since all are born in Adam and are justified in Christ. As long as people remain sinners in the flesh, in need of forgiveness, there is much to say in God's stead.

The Gospel is not merely information, but a release from the wrath of God and the penalty of sin. However, the need for this absolution must be wrought by a fully condemning law. Where the law is minimized, so is the Gospel, and vice versa. "Luther was always deeply conscious of the wrath of God as a terrible, continuing reality."[13] The reality of the law is undercut when a universal Gospel, outside of Christ, is assumed, but what is needed, when the law cuts to the heart properly, "is not a mere reminder of forgiveness, but the thing itself."[14]

To limit the Gospel is to be ashamed of it, whatever the motivation. To deny the objective aspect of justification colors Christ's work ineffective and His atonement weak, so that man must complete it today by his actions or works. The completeness of redemption is evident, though, and was made publicly known in the Father's raising of the Son, who bore our sins, so that "he has made satisfaction and received forgiveness on our behalf."[15]

---

[13] Kurt Marquart, "Reformation Roots of Objective Justification," 126.

[14] Kurt Marquart, "Reformation Roots of Objective Justification," 127.

[15] Magnus Sørensen, "The Justification of Christ," 31.

Chapter 23

Conclusion

Controversy clarifies doctrinal stances. New words are often chosen to make more careful distinctions between God's truth and human error. The teaching of justification is supposedly made simple by its deniers, but, in wiping out the tension between law and Gospel, they let false logical inferences rule out the full truth of Scripture. The faithful Christian must hold to and hear these two messages, even when they seem to be at odds: God is angry at sin and does not accept it, but, in Christ, all sin is forgiven and the world is reconciled to Him.

This is a far more necessary distinction than ever—in the wake of a new error that denies the completeness and effectiveness of Christ's work. One's stance on this topic determines what is preached and how the Gospel is defined. It is a crucial matter, though it has been burdened with pointless controversy and unhelpful polemics. It is not the human words in themselves that matter, but the divine teaching the inspired Scriptures give us. Due to historical errors, our language gradually becomes more precise. This has always been the case for the church on earth: when biblical language is perverted, outside words must safeguard the scriptural doctrine. It is not enough to simply repeat biblical phrases, thinking the matter is settled.

That does not mean that every statement under the guise of objective justification is correct. Care must be taken to conform our teaching to God's Word. Sinful logic wants to say: If the world is redeemed, every person is thereby redeemed. This is devilish false doctrine. So it is also with objective justification—it must be determined by Scripture, not what logic makes it say. The Bible—most lucidly in 2 Cor. 5:19—speaks of the effect of Christ's work from God's side. It is not the only biblical vantage point or way of speaking, but it certainly is a necessary one that should be confessed boldly in the face of those who would make personal faith the replacement for Christ's resurrection.

As the Reformers confessed the role of works in regard to faith much clearer than those who went before them, so modern Lutherans have the opportunity to confess clearly the basis and extent of salvation—the absolution of the whole world in Christ that empowers the Gospel message—due to the infiltration of a new satanic error, which denies that Christ's atonement is effective before faith comes to an individual. "The underscoring of the universal justification [of the world] is necessary in order to preserve the real content of the Gospel."[1]

In this age where words multiply and there is much eloquent talk about the law and the Gospel, there is a real failure to actually use these simultaneous divine powers that are both in effect. This is due to a doctrinal deficiency, or perhaps just cowardice. Where there is nothing to preach, nothing will be taught. " . . . in this controversy the chief topic of Christian doctrine is treated, which, understood aright, illumines and amplifies the honor of Christ, and brings necessary and most abundant consolation to devout consciences. . . . " (Ap 4:2).

A sermon should not be merely a talk about forgiveness or the Christian life, but God's voice of wrath to condemn sin and Christ's all-powerful forgiveness to take away sins. The Gospel has the inherent power of forgiveness, by virtue of Christ's absolution of our sin. It is not to be safeguarded from sinners who will trample it, but used indiscriminately—not in place of the law, but in biblical coordination.

The scriptural doctrine, no matter how offensive, must be defended at all costs: "How is it that the consciousness that the Evangelical Lutheran Church alone is entrusted with the pure doctrine of justification has largely disappeared even within this our church?" The answer to this question is a wake-up call: "Because most of the teachers in it have themselves lost this treasure."[2] Communicating the Gospel is not only

---

[1] Adolf Hoenecke, quoted in: Kurt Marquart, "Objective Justification," *Marquart's Works*, 6:93.

[2] Walther, *Essays for the Church*, 1:54.

a matter of the right language or traditional phrasing, but preserving the power of the world's absolution in Christ and actually using and believing it: "The greatest honor you can bestow on God and his keys is to trust in them."[3]

> *Christ Jesus, God's own Son, came down . . .*
> *Destroying sin He took the crown From Death's*
> *pale brow forever; Stripped of pow'r, no more it*
> *reigns; An empty form alone remains; Its sting is*
> *lost forever. Alleluia!*
>
> *. . . Christ alone our souls will feed; He is our*
> *meat and drink indeed; Faith lives upon no other!*
> *Alleluia!*[4]

---

[3]Luther, "The Keys" (1530), LW 40:368.

[4]Martin Luther, "Christ Jesus Lay in Death's Strong Bands," *Lutheran Service Book* (St. Louis: CPH, 2006), Hymn 458.

Selected References

Association of Confessional Lutheran Churches, The. "Critique of the Evangelical Lutheran Diocese of North America's Theses on Justification." Feb. 9, 2014. http://www.dropbox.com/s/rczja2b8f2k9jgf/ACLC-Official_Critique_of_ELDoNA_Theses_on_Justification.pdf.

Barrow, Isaac. "The Christian Faith Explained and Vindicated." *The Works of Isaac Barrow.* Volume 2. Edited by Abraham Hill and James Hamilton. New York: John C. Riker, 1845. http://archive.org/details/worksofisaacbarr02barr.

Becker, Siegbert W. "Objective Justification." Chicago Pastoral Conference, WELS, Elgin, Illinois. Nov. 9, 1982. http://essays.wls.wels.net/bitstream/handle/123456789/331/BeckerJustification.pdf.

Buchholz, Jon D. "Jesus Canceled Your Debt!" 2012. http://essays.wls.wels.net/bitstream/handle/123456789/950/BuchholzJustification.pdf.

Calov, Abraham. "Thoughts on Objective Justification: Selections from Abraham Calov's *Biblia Illustrata*: 2 Corinthians 5:18–19; Romans 3:23–24, 4:25, and 5:18–19." Translated by Souksamay K. Phetsanghane. Southwestern Conference of the Western Wisconsin District of the Wisconsin Evangelical Lutheran Synod, Winter Conference, Baraboo, WI. Feb. 25, 2014. http://essays.wls.wels.net/handle/123456789/989.

Commission on Theology and Church Relations, "Theses on Justification." The Lutheran Church–Missouri Synod. May, 1983. http://www.lcms.org/Document.fdoc?src=lcm&id=422.

Curia, Rick Nicholas. *The Significant History of the Doctrine of Objective or Universal Justification among the Churches of the Former Evangelical Lutheran Synodical Conference of North America.* 1983. http://archive.org/details/TheSignificantHistoryOfTheDoctrineOfObjectiveOrUniversalJustification.

Diers, Martin W. "Objective Justification: The Controversy Examined." 2013 Convocation of the Orthodox Lutheran Confessional Conference. http://lutherantheology.com/uploads/works/papers/ObjectiveJustification_2013_mwd.pdf.

Evangelical Lutheran Diocese of North America. "Theses on the Article of Justification as Taught in Holy Scripture and the Confessions of Christ's Holy

Church with Special Attention to 'Objective Justification'." 2013 Colloquium and Synod.
http://www.eldona.org/ELDoNA/Papers_files/Justification_2013.pdf.

Franzmann, Martin H. "Reconciliation and Justification." *Concordia Theological Monthly* XXI:2. Feb. 1950.
http://www.ctsfw.net/media/pdfs/FranzmannReconciliationJustification.pdf.

Hardt, Tom G. A. "Justification and Easter: A Study in Subjective and Objective Justification in Lutheran Theology." *A Lively Legacy: Essays in Honor of Robert Preus.* Edited by Kurt E. Marquart, John R. Stephenson, and Bjarne W. Teigen. Fort Wayne: Concordia Theological Seminary Press, 1985.
http://luk.se/Justification-Easter.htm.

Harley, Vernon H. "Synergism—Its Logical Association with General or Universal Justification." 1984.
http://ichabodthegloryhasdeparted.blogspot.com/2015/12/synergism-its-logical-association-with.html.

Huber, Samuel. "Samuel Huber on Election and Justification: Translations from His Writings." Translated by Andrew Hussman. April 26, 2013. http://essays.wls.wels.net/bitstream/handle/123456789/2282/Huber%20Translations_0.pdf.

Humberger, John. *Absolution; or Forgiveness of Sins: Established by the Holy Scriptures.* Tract. No. 5. Columbus, OH: Lutheran Book Concern, 1880. Reprint, Omaha, NE: Mercinator Press, 2019.

Jackson, Gregory L. *Luther versus the Pietists: Justification by Faith.* Martin Chemnitz Press. Revised, 2012.

Korthals, James F. "Universal/Objective Justification: An Historical Perspective." Kettle Moraine Pastoral Conference, West Mequon, WI. Jan. 15 2013.
http://essays.wls.wels.net/bitstream/handle/123456789/4143/KorthalsJustification.pdf.

Luther, Martin. "The Keys." *Luther's Works: Church and Ministry II.* Volume 40:325–394. Edited by Helmut T. Lehmann and Conrad Bergendoff. St. Louis: Concordia Publishing House, 1958.

Maier [II], Walter A. "A Summary Exposition of the Doctrine of Justification by Grace Through Faith." 1981. http://www.wlsessays.net/bitstream/handle/123456789/3210/MaierJustification.pdf.

Marquart, Kurt E. *Marquart's Works: Justification.* Volume VI of X. Edited by Herman J. Otten. New Haven, MO: Lutheran News, 2014–15.

———. "The Reformation Roots of Objective Justification." *A Lively Legacy: Essays in Honor of Robert Preus.* Edited by Kurt E. Marquart, John R. Stephenson, and Bjarne W. Teigen. Fort Wayne: Concordia Theological Seminary Press, 1985. http://www.ctsfw.net/media/pdfs/MarquartReformationRootsofObjectiveJustification.pdf.

Meyer, Heinrich August Wilhelm. *Critical and Exegetical Hand book to the Epistles to the Corinthians.* New York: Funk and Wagnalls, 1884.
http://play.google.com/books/reader?id=FkRDAAAAYAAJ.

Pieper, Franz. "C.F.W. Walther as Theologian: Justification, Universal." *Lehre und Wehre*. Feb. 1890. Translated by Wallace McLaughlin. http://backtoluther.blogspot.com/2013/02/walther-as-theologian-justification-by_28.html.

Preus, Robert D. "Justification as Taught by Post-Reformation Lutheran Theologians." March 26, 1982. http://archive.org/details/JustificationAsTaughtByPost-reformationLutheranTheologians.

———. "Objective Justification." *Concordia Theological Seminary Newsletter*. Spring 1981. http://www.angelfire.com/ny4/djw/PreusJustification.html.

———, ed. "Selected Articles on Objective Justification." Fort Wayne: Concordia Theological Seminary Press. http://www.angelfire.com/ny4/djw/ObjectiveJustificationArticles.pdf.

Preuss, Edward. *Justification of the Sinner before God*. Translated by J. A. Friedrich. *Theological Monthly*. 1928–29. Reprint, Fort Wayne: Concordia Theological Seminary Press, 1970. Reprint, Lutheran Legacy, 2011.

Rydecki, Paul. "On Francis Pieper's Misuse of Romans 4:25 as a Biblical Basis for Objective Justification." Colloquium of the Evangelical Lutheran Diocese of North America, Fort Wayne, IN. Jan. 16, 2018. http://www.godwithuslc.org/wp-content/uploads/2018/02/On-Pieper-and-Romans-4_2017.pdf.

———. "The Forensic Appeal to the Throne of Grace in the Theology of the Lutheran Age of Orthodoxy: A Reflection on Atonement and its Relationship to Justification." Colloquium of the Evangelical Lutheran Diocese of North America, Malone, Texas. April 30, 2013. http://eldona.org/ELDoNA/Papers_files/ForensicAppeal_Rydecki_Final.pdf.

Smeaton, George. *The Doctrine of the Atonement as Taught by the Apostles; or the Sayings of the Apostles Exegetically Expounded*. Edinburgh: T & T Clark, 1870. http://archive.org/details/doctrineofatonem00smea.

———. *The Doctrine of the Atonement as Taught by Christ Himself*. Edinburgh: T & T Clark. 2nd ed., 1871. Reprint, Grand Rapids: Zondervan, 1953. http://archive.org/details/docofatone00smeauoft.

Sørensen, Magnus N. "The Justification of Christ as the Efficient Cause of our Justification—the Narrow Lutheran Middle in the Controversy on Universal Objective Justification." 2017 Convocation of the Orthodox Lutheran Confessional Conference. http://www.academia.edu/34121363/The_Justification_of_Christ_as_the_Efficient_Cause_of_Our_Justification_-The_Narrow_Lutheran_Middle_in_the_Controversy_on_Universal_Objective_Justification.

———. "Theses on Universal Objective Justification." 2018 Convocation of the Orthodox Lutheran Confessional Conference.

Sullivan, Joshua "Objective Justification." Four parts. *Ask the Pastor*. 2015. http://www.youtube.com/watch?v=O-y90Eqwx-Y.

Stoeckhardt, George. "General Justification." Translated by Otto F. Stahlke. *CTQ* 42:2. April 1978.
http://ctsfwmedia.s3.amazonaws.com/CTQ/CTQ%2042-2.pdf.

Tankersley, Lee. "Raised for Our Justification: The Resurrection and Penal Substitution." *The Southern Baptist Journal of Theology* 18:4. Winter 2014. http://equip.sbts.edu/publications/journals/journal-of-theology/raised-for-our-justification-the-resurrection-and-penal-substitution.

Walther, C.F.W. *Justification—Objective and Subjective: A Translation of the Doctrinal Essay Read at the First Convention of the Synodical Conference in 1872.* Translated by Kurt Marquart. Fort Wayne: Concordia Theological Seminary Press. http:
//www.angelfire.com/ny4/djw/JustificationObjectiveSubjectiveMarquart.pdf.

Warth, Martim C. "Justification through Faith in Article Four of the Apology." *CTQ* 46:2–3. April–July 1982.
http://www.ctsfw.net/media/pdfs/warthjustification.pdf.

Webber, David Jay. "Our Righteousness before God . . . is Revealed in the Gospel. On this Righteousness Faith Relies." The Emmaus Conference. Tacoma, Washington. April 22-23, 2015.
http://www.angelfire.com/ny4/djw/WebberEmmausConferenceEssay.pdf.

www.ingramcontent.com/pod-product-compliance
Lightning Source LLC
Chambersburg PA
CBHW060013050426

42448CB00012B/2736